Will We be Brilliant or What?

SONGS AND STORIES

John Spillane has enjoyed over thirty-three years of an ever-consistent, illuminating and exciting career within the world of music. He continues to tour all around the world and has been awarded Meteor Irish Music Awards for Best Folk Act and Best Traditional Act.

www.johnspillane.ie
www.facebook.com/john.spillane.musician.ireland
twitter.com/JohnSpillane09
itunes.apple.com/ie/artist/john-spillane/id69908695

Will we be Brilliant or What?

SONGS AND STORIES

JOHN SPILLANE

Foreword by CHRISTY MOORE

The Collins Press

FIRST PUBLISHED IN 2016 BY
The Collins Press
West Link Park
Doughcloyne
Wilton
Cork
T12N5EF
Ireland

© John Spillane 2016

Lyrics and music to all songs © John Spillane, unless otherwise credited

A CIP record for this book is available from the British Library.

Paperback ISBN: 978-1-84889-2859

Book design and guitar motif illustration by
Anú Design, Tara

Typesetting by Patricia Hope
Typeset in AGaramond and Grotesk
Printed in Malta by Gutenberg Press Limited

CONTENTS

Foreword by Christy Moore   xi

Introduction   1

Part One. ***Where the Wind Runs her Fingers above the Dark Lee***

    Prince's Street   7

    My Love Will not Sing for Me   11

    The Land You Love the Best   14

    My First Band, My First Gig   16

    Ghosts   22

    The Only One for Me   24

    The Stargazers   26

    I Won't Be Afraid Any More   30

    Nomos   33

    All the Ways You Wander   36

Part Two. ***Everything's Turning to Gold, Cathy***

    Everything's Turning to Gold, Cathy   41

    We're Going Sailing   44

    It Wasn't to Be   47

Not too Bad   50

When You and I Were True   52

I'm Going to Set You Free   56

Meet Me on the Midnight Shore   59

The Poor Weary Wanderer   62

A Songwriting Workshop. Right Now!   65

Part Three. *Will We Be All Dressed in Sunlight?*

Will We Be Brilliant or What?   69

Magic Nights in the Lobby Bar   72

The Dance of the Cherry Trees   75

Let the River Flow   79

The Madwoman of Cork   82

Orca, Orca, Killer Whale   88

The Moon Going Home   94

Hey Dreamer   96

Cork   98

I'm Moving On   100

The Wild Flowers   102

There Was a Man Who Took a Wife   104

Gortatagort   107

Rise Up, Lovely Molly   111

The Dunnes Stores Girl   114

Part Four. *The River to the Stars Confessed*

Passage West   119

The Ballad of Patrick Murphy   122

The Ferry Arms   126

The Voyage of the *Sirius*   130

Lovers' Leap   134

Folklore and Mythology   139

A Rock To Cling To   141

The Dancer   144

When We Sang   147

My Lovely Smiling Beamish Boy   150

The Irish Language   153

Martin's Mad About Fish   156

River Lee   157

The English Market Christmas Angel Song   160

Part Five. *Spillane the Wanderer from Town to Town*

Johnny, Don't Go to Ballincollig   167

Beautiful Ballincollig   171

Life in an Irish Town   177

Graiguenamanagh   180

Fethard Town   182

Castleisland   185

Kiltimagh – The Dark Wind from the Mountain   188

Some Cover Versions   190

Near Cootehill Town   193

Castlepollard – At the Very Heart of Ireland   195

Boyle –The Man Who Came In From the Dark   197

Kells – When Colm Cille Was a Boy   201

Gorey – A Song for Myles Byrne   203

Baile Átha an Rí – Athenry   206

Killaloe – There Was a King in Ireland   209

Youghal   212

Molly Bawn O'Leary from the County Tipperary   214

The Streets of Ballyphehane   217

Farewell   220

Foreword

My first contact with John Spillane was in 1993 when my brother Andy brought me a cassette of John's songs from Cork city. In 1997 I got a copy of John's first solo album, *The Wells of The World*. I fell beneath its spell. Since then we have been in regular contact. Our primary interest has always been the writing and singing of ballads.

As two working balladeers we collaborate together and support each other as best we can. John's songs have become a precious part of my repertoire. In particular, 'Gortatagort' and 'Magic Nights in The Lobby Bar' are among my favourite songs in a lifetime spent singing.

In recent years John's songs have become an inspiration to singers worldwide. Here at home in Ireland, his excellent series of programmes on TG4, *Spillane an Fánaí*, provides insights into the ancient tradition of ballads in Ireland.

Singers need songs and songwriters need singers . . . John Spillane excels in both fields. I will cherish this book, as I do his friendship.

Christy Moore

Introduction

Gentle reader, this book is a collection of songs that I have made up myself, out of my imagination. Fair play to me. I hope you will enjoy my songs and stories. Thanks to my wife Cathy, my daughter Leslie, and all my family. Thanks to my manager Lorcan Ennis, and to all the great musicians, writers and head-the-balls I've had the privilege of hanging out with all these years. Rock on lads, rock on! Thank you, thank you all!

I fell in love with singing when I was a small boy, and used to wander around the footpaths of Cork chanting away quietly to myself. 'My Bonnie Lies over the Ocean' was the first song I fell in love with as a child, and I remember being fascinated by the way it was put together, the order of the words, the pattern of the lines and the tune. I was four years old that time, a great age, when I fell in love with singing.

I went to school in a fabulous place called St Joseph's on the Mardyke in Cork. At the back of the school flowed the River Lee, all beautiful, with a great flock of swans. That magical stretch of the river between the Green Bridge and the Shaky Bridge was our playground. We never really learned music at school, except for lots of singing, and we used to go to the City Hall every year to sing in the Cór Fhéile na Scol.

One time, however, we were visited by a man with a guitar, who sang us 'Weela Weela Waile', which frightened the life out of us with its story of the old woman who lived in the wood – 'she stuck the penknife in the baby's heart, a weela weela waile'. We also learned 'The Old Woman from Wexford' from our teacher, Mr Goggin. That one was about poisoning and drowning. Murder and mayhem and dying for Ireland were features of many of the songs of my childhood.

Another time, a man came in and taught us the scale, the 'do re mi'. He showed us how to move up and down that musical ladder, and how you could jump to any note you wanted when you got the hang of it. That music lesson has stood to me all my life and I still think in terms of the 'do re mi', even though I can read and write music now and play some magical chords on the guitar!

My dad died when I was one and a half years old, in August 1962, and left my mother with five small boys, the oldest nearly seven and the youngest only six months. My mother had a lot on her hands and she used to put us on the bus down to Bantry, to her home place, the farm, for the school holidays: Christmas, Easter and summer. Our uncle Tim, my hero, the farmer, was there, with our Grandma. We loved the farm. It was a second home for us. That was a very different world from the streetlights of the semi-detached suburbs we came from in Wilton, Cork. That was dark and wild country, in the west Cork hills. There were no footpaths there or streetlights, and every morning we went for the cows and carried the milk to the churns. There was a lot of singing done on the farm, milking the cows, in the fields and around the turf fire at night. Republican ballads were all the rage – 'The Lonely Woods of Upton', 'Down by the Glenside', 'An Irish Soldier Laddie' – lots of songs.

When I was fifteen I was sent to the Gaeltacht to learn Irish, at Ballingeary in west Cork, a most beautiful and enchanting place. We were bunked in with a crowd from Dublin, and one of them, a lad called Sponger, had a guitar and gave me my first lesson. He taught me 'Brain Damage' by Pink Floyd. That's where I caught the guitar bug. As soon as I got home, I tore into my brother Mossie's guitar, an old banger he got with the Green Shield Stamps. That guitar only had two strings, and I learned a whole lot of music with my two-string style. The idea of the full six strings still excites me!

Learning guitar is an exciting journey. It's good to have an ol' path to follow, in life, like.

I wrote my first song when I was sixteen and I have written about 200 songs since then. Some of them maybe you couldn't really call brilliant songs, like, but what harm? Each one teaches you some little lesson, and maybe you have to write the small ones so you can go on and write the big ones. Anyway, I believe that the best is yet to come and now that I am kind of getting the hang of it, I think there are some beauties of songs out there waiting to fall into my lap! Dream on, Johnny boy, dream on! Anyway, they say that everyone has a book in them, so this is mine and I hope you enjoy it, gentle reader.

Thank you and rock on!

John Spillane,
Passage West,
County Cork

PART ONE

Where the Wind Runs her Fingers

above the Dark Lee

Prince's Street

I spent Monday on Strawberry Hill,
Till I fell and I landed on your windowsill,
I hung there by a golden fine web,
I had woven from a hair of your head.

I spent Tuesday just walking through town,
Till I saw a gold angel come tumbling down.
And waltzing with seagulls up in an elm tree,
Where the wind runs her fingers above the dark Lee.

And oh will you meet me on Saturday night?
We'll dance in the shadows between the street lights.
Between these two rivers I know where we'll meet,
On Prince's Street.

I spent Wednesday doing nothing at all,
Till late in the evening the wind came to call,

And stood at my window and danced a handstand,
The sun on her shoulder and birds in her hands.

The next morning I woke from a dream,
Of where the fish lie on their beds of deep green,
I watched Thursday morning put on its new coat,
Of cloud at the elbow, blue sky at the throat.

And oh will you meet me on Saturday night?
We'll dance in the shadows between the street lights.
Between these two rivers I know where we'll meet,
On Prince's Street.

I spent Friday just counting the time,
Till up in a tower I heard some bells chime,
I saw a great goldfish take wing like a swan,
And told me that Saturday wouldn't be long.

And oh will you meet me on Saturday night?
We'll dance in the shadows between the street lights.
Between these two rivers I know where we'll meet,
On Prince's Street.

And oh will you meet me on Saturday night?
We'll dance with your ankles all bathed in moonlight,
Between these two rivers I know where we'll meet,
On Prince's Street.

I wrote 'Prince's Street' when I was twenty-two years old. It just came to me. I was busking for a while with my friend Nuala on Prince's Street at that time and I was learning Irish. I looked up at the sign and I saw Prince's Street – *Sráid an Phrionsa*, the Street of the Prince. Seeing it in the Irish conjured up this image of the prince in a way the English didn't. At that time I was also serving a musical apprenticeship with musician Noel Shine from County Clare. I learned a lot of folk and traditional tunes from Noel, who lived at the top of Strawberry Hill. It was nice to be strolling down Strawberry Hill on a sunny morning with the city stretched out below you like a playground, like a great carnival.

I suppose I was trying to capture the magic feeling of the special, lovely places around Cork city, especially along the river and up around St Finbarr's Cathedral, where the gold angel of the resurrection hangs out. I've always felt Cork to have a special magic. I remember an incredibly sunny day when I was small and we were taken out of school on the Mardyke and over to St Finbarr's Cathedral, where we were shown the angel and told the story: two times that angel has fallen down from its perch, and the next time it will fall will be on the last day, at the end of the world.

I wrote this song in the very early 1980s. I was not in tune with the musical trend at the time, which was new-wave punk. A lot of the other songwriters around were attacking Cork big time, and the repressive, dark, small-minded mentality they saw there. Funny how different people can look at the same thing and see completely different things.

So anyway, I wrote the song and what I wasn't even thinking about, or conscious of, was that of course my father and all his family were reared on Prince's Street, in number fourteen, over a shop. That was before I was born. I must have been aware of it, on some level. So it is a song for my dad, who died when I was one and a half, and I didn't even realise it when I was writing it. I often feel the best songs are the ones that just come to you. They float down from the air; you are kind of like a channel, or an aerial.

This was my biggest and best song for years, and it took me a long time to get beyond it. I get a lot of requests for it, usually from people who are around the age I was when I wrote it. They get it.

I played in a great band called The Stargazers from 1984 to 1991, with my friends Johnny (Fang) Murphy and Chris Ahern. We played mostly swing music in three-part harmony from the golden era of American songwriting, the 1930s and '40s – songs by the likes of Irving Berlin, Cole Porter, Hoagy Carmichael. I was trying to swing us over into doing original material as well, and in 1989 we released an acapella version of 'Prince's Street' as a single, which got a lot of airplay at the time. Happy days in the Hit Factory.

My Love Will not Sing for Me

My love will not sing for me, she cannot find the time,
She sits among the tables, drinking blood-red wine.

She calls me to her sometimes, I go swimming in her hair,
She's got mad blue eyes, that swallow when she stares.

And I need her like I need a Mercedes-Benz,
Like I need another drink, do you think,
You could see your way to helping me, my friend?
See your way to helping me, my friend?

All I really want from you, is a sympathetic ear,
Someone who could buy me one more pint of beer,

And I'll tell you about my broken heart, I'll tell it just for you,
No one ever had a heart as broken as I do.

And I need her like I need a Mercedes-Benz,
Like I need another drink, do you think,
You could see your way to helping me, my friend?
See your way to helping me, my friend?

My love will not sing for me, she cannot find the time,
She sits among the tables, drinking blood-red wine.

I was twenty-one years old when I wrote this song, and it was a breakthrough song for me at that time. A breakthrough song is one that is bigger and better than anything you have written before. If you keep at it and use your imagination, you will surely get a breakthrough song eventually. As my mother used to say, 'With patience and perseverance, you could bring a donkey from Kinsale to Jerusalem.' I had written quite a few songs by the time I wrote this one, but this is the first of them to make it into this book.

I remember I had the chords and the first verse for a long time, but could get no further. Then I got a gig! I was to play support to Jimmy MacCarthy in Garry's Inn in Cork, where he played every Sunday night. Jimmy was a big hero of mine, and a brilliant songwriter. I was very worked-up about playing before him, and also very anxious to impress. Well, the night before the gig, I sat down and finished the whole song in one go, in about five minutes, verses, chorus and all. There was a little lesson there. The gigging and the songwriting are very different things, but one can help the other. I am always looking for ways forward, little lessons, tricks of the trade, which I am happy to pass on to you, gentle reader!

The song was inspired by a girl who told me that I had 'no hope whatsoever of making it in music'. She could not be with me because of the life of poverty she would have with me. She was going to marry the money! I hope she found what she was looking for. Meanwhile, I have enjoyed a successful life in music and many bright and shining adventures on the sea of life.

Another little lesson, gentle reader – don't ever let anybody put you down!

This was the first song I got recorded and released. It was on a radio show and an album called *The Best of Sounds Promising* on RTÉ Records. I performed it with my friend Noel Shine. I got my first royalty money from this song, and it made me feel like royalty. It still earns a few bob, and who knows, maybe it will be the big song in the end, when all is said and done!

The Land You Love the Best

When angels with wings come to collect you,
To carry you over the stormy sea,
Whispering things, as they caress you,
Gently they'll press you, with sweet words undress you;

'Will you lie in the land that holds you and keeps you,
Or the land you love the best?
The land you love the best, the land you love the best,
Will you lie in the garden of peace and of order,
Or the cold wild field in the west?'

When night and her shadows come to surround you,
To touch you with fingers of cold, cold fear.
When the voice of the stranger echoes around you,
When strange words confound you, strange accents
    drown you;

'Will you fly to the land that fed you and found you,
Or the land you love the best?
The land you love the best, the land you love the best,
Will you lie in the garden of peace and of order,
Or the cold wild field in the west?'

This song was inspired by my aunty Frances. She lived in London for about forty years, working for Shell Oil Company. I visited her when I was over playing a gig with The Stargazers in 1992. She had retired and lived in Kensington. I was trying to persuade her to move back to Cork, where she had relations, and not to spend her retirement alone in London. She said she didn't think she could ever live in Cork again, because they were so poor there when she was a child. She loved England now, and London, and besides, our Taoiseach was a gangster. When I got home, I wrote this song, which is kind of a continuation of our conversation. So many Irish people have gone to live in other lands. They have escaped to newer, better places. I remember a song I heard when I was a kid called 'Will My Soul Pass Through Old Ireland?' which had a similar theme. 'The Land' has been covered by quite a few people, including a lovely version by Mary Greene and Noel Shine, and also by that great Galway singer Seán Keane.

Frances was a lovely lady. She passed away a few years ago, the last of her brothers and sisters. She used to speak very lovingly of the farm in Bantry where they all came from (I call it 'the cold wild field in the west') and would sometimes quote lines from 'The Old Bog Road' by Teresa Brayton:

Had I the chance to wander back, or own a king's abode,
'Tis soon I'd see the hawthorn tree, by the Old Bog Road.

My First Band, My First Gig

When I was a child, I thought being a musician was something totally beyond reach. I didn't know any musicians, and I never thought in a million years that I would or could ever become one myself. I didn't play any musical instrument or have any training whatsoever. I mean, we learned a little bit of tin whistle at school, and maybe messed around with a mouth organ, but none of us knew how to play them really. When I was young I wanted to be a writer, as I was good at writing compositions, and often my stories would be read out by the teacher. I did love to sing. I loved singing, and down in Bantry, on the farm, I learned that the old songs were treated with huge reverence and respect, and that there was a kind of musical geography going on; we were singing about other parts of Ireland, and comparing each place according to its songs. There were rock operas at our school every year, put on by a brilliant character called Tony Doherty or The Doc. Tony was a teacher, but he brought us all out climbing mountains, and had us putting on rock operas. When I was in second year of secondary school, I was in a musical called *Holy Moses*, and I was picked out of the crowd for a solo because my voice was ringing out good and clear, but shortly afterwards that voice broke and disappeared forever. The song was 'Freedom! From the Iron Hand of the Pharaoh!' I'll never forget it; I fell in love with the smell of the greasepaint, the thrill of the first night, the fall of the curtain. The next year, I got a lead part as one of the children of Lir; I was a singing swan. Those shows were brilliant excitement and I'll always be grateful to The Doc for putting me on the stage.

Then I learned my first two guitar chords in the Ballingeary Gaeltacht and I was off. And then I met Tony Buckley from up the road, and, sitting on the wall at the corner of the park one dark night, he taught me the most wonderful and beautiful chord called A Minor. Oh my god! A Minor! Bow down, ladies and gentlemen! What an amazing phenomenon of a chord; angels sing when you strum that chord called A Minor. Learning to play the guitar was the beginning of a fabulous journey. Neil Young music was all the rage on the guitar at that time in the 1970s, especially 'The Needle and the Damage Done', which was a big show-off number. I started to learn the guitar when I was fifteen, and by the time I was twenty I was a professional musician.

I had a friend from down the road as well, called Dave Murphy. Dave could play piano really well, and sing and make up songs, which was phenomenal. He could be sitting right next to you, but when he played piano and sang, he seemed to disappear into a complete world of his own. One day I had an idea – a light came on in my head – and that was to get Dave and Tony and myself to try and play something together. Well, that was the start of the band – it went on for years after that. That's what started all the trouble, like!

We jammed away like mad for the next few years, down in Dave's house playing guitars into a tape recorder, or up in Tony's bedroom, or in the shed at the back of my house. There was fierce activity and we had a brilliant time. We got Niall Marron in on the drums and we were a band then. Dave came up with the name: Bootlace.

I wrote my first song in the autumn of my sixth year at secondary school. I had written a few smaller pieces before that, but this was a fully finished song. It was called 'The Leaves Are Golden Brown'. It was a sad love song about being deserted by the one you love. It had never happened to me at all; I was just making it up, but it happened to me later on, alright.

> The leaves are golden brown, as they tumble down
>   from the clear autumn sky,
> My love has gone away, said she couldn't stay, left
>   me here with a lie.

We played our first gig at our own graduation dance, when we were seventeen. The main band took a break and we went on for about six songs. We were a bit drunk, but lashed it out grand. I remember singing 'Johnny B. Goode' by Chuck Berry. Afterwards one of the main band came over to me for a chat and told me, 'Ye were very good, but never forget one thing – there's only one Rory Gallagher.' I didn't grasp his meaning at first, but then I got it – he was telling me not to get my hopes up, I was never going to make it! Wow! First time out and that's what I got told.

Christmas came, and Tony got on to me about a suss he had on getting a few bob for playing in a pub called O'Neill's on Barrack Street on Christmas Eve. I remember having to ask my mother if I could do it. Off we went with two guitars, a little amp, a mike and stand, and completely bluffed it. Tony had a few Eagles songs, but I think I was just reading a few ballads out of a book. I remember 'Three Times a Lady' was a hit at the time and we chanced our arms at a version of it a few times. I learned that night that it is just amazing how much people love music. They go all happy. It's fascinating what you can get away with too, if you have enough neck! As the night went on, everybody got completely drunk, and there was about an inch of beer on the pub floor. Then an almighty fight broke out, digs were thrown and this huge, locked fellah got stretched out on the ground. The guards were called and an ambulance arrived, lights flashing, sirens blaring. The whole thing fell completely to pieces: murder and mayhem. That's the first gig I did that I got paid for – the first money I earned from playing music.

When we all did the Leaving Cert and finished school, I vowed that whatever else I was going to do, I definitely was not going to college, because I was completely fed up of books and never wanted to open another textbook as long as I lived. Those teenage years locked in school learning boring stuff you were always going to forget seemed such a waste of time; we could have been out running wild and free in the woods and meadows, like Huckleberry Finn, or playing music! Just a few days after my eighteenth birthday, I got a job in the bank: the Bank of Ireland, the Bank of a Lifetime! In those days, you applied for the bank, the Civil Service and the ESB, and I got the bank.

I was up in Limerick working in the bank for two years, and every weekend I was down practising with the band. We started to do a few gigs around the country as well. We changed name from Bootlace to Sabre, and got a residency playing in Sir Henry's rock café in Cork every Wednesday. I'd be up to Limerick on the train Thursday morning, and hitch from Limerick Junction into work, in the back door of the bank.

The band was getting serious and we were deadly passionate about it. Niall left, and we got Sam O'Sullivan and later Art Lorigan on drums. But it was me, Tony and Dave who were the band, really. The problem was we were really like three bands. We had too many chiefs and not enough Indians. Anyway, we were getting better and we really loved it. We bought a Ford Transit van and a PA system on hire purchase, and started travelling a bit. Then we got a manager and we lost the head altogether. Tony was working in Hibernian Insurance, and he and I started talking about giving up our jobs and going full-time. We wanted to do something we loved. I have to say, I really enjoyed working in the bank and all the people I met there. They were grand people. Anyway, we went for it. We made a PACT! We were going to go in on Monday morning and hand in our resignations. We were young. The world was our oyster. I wrote a poetic letter of resignation to my manager, something about going in search of 'fresh pastures new'. I was shaking as I handed it to him. The assistant manager asked me to rewrite it; it was too flowery. I didn't. I got into the lift. I was going down to the safe. I met an older, very respectable colleague, and says he to me, 'Good for you, boy. I wish I got out years ago. I got trapped and I can never leave.'

Those words always stayed with me. The poor man. I knew that if I didn't get out young I'd never get out. You get caught. You think about your whole life working in the bank. And who was the bank? 'It's not me, it's the bank', they'd say. But who was the bank? You could dig as deep as you wanted and go as high as you could, and you would never get to the bank. As Woody Guthrie sang:

As through this world I've wandered, I've seen lots
   of funny men,
Some will rob you with a six-gun, and some with
   a fountain pen.

We went professional. We did gigs in Wicklow, Cork, Dublin, Carlow, Wexford, Tralee, Castlegregory, Midleton, Clonmel, Limerick. It was a brilliant time, but the problem was we were not getting on with each other. There was a power struggle. We were fighting all the time, and then we split up. Such a pity that we were not able to strike a balance between us. That was my first band, and when I left it I walked away by myself into the darkness. Those were stormy days, being young in Ireland in 1982.

Ghosts

It had to happen, as these things do,
That the ghost of me would meet the ghost of you,
In the shadows of this haunted town,
As the night came floating down,
You look through me, I look through you,
What do you see when you see right through?

You see nothing, nothing but empty,
Promises of plenty,
Promises of you, promises of you.

It had to happen, as these things do,
That the ghost of me would meet the ghost of you,
By some thin thread that did not fall,
When we thought love had broken all,
We thought love had broken all.

And left nothing, nothing but empty,
Promises of plenty,
Promises of you, promises of you.

It had to happen, as these things do,
That the ghost of me would meet the ghost of you,
In the shadows of this haunted town,
As the night came floating down.

I met someone from my past who I had been close to but had not seen for years. I met them on Patrick's Hill in the dusky twilight. There was nothing to say, and we both passed on, like ghosts. I wrote this song about that sad old feeling.

The Only One for Me

It's been ten long years since the boy went singing
To his true love's door,
Crying 'Oh my true love, let me in'
Ten long years or more.

Down she comes with her falling hair,
Comes to let him in,
Comes to show him a secret light, burning.

'You're the only one for me,
You're the only one for me,
And you'll always be
The only one for me.'

Now the boy walks in stony silence,
His hollow footsteps ring,

Along the streets where he once went spinning,
Loving everything.
Now the footprints of crows and sparrows
Gather 'round his eyes,
Now the weight of the world has cut him
Down to size.

'You're the only one for me,
You're the only one for me,
And you'll always be
The only one for me.'

It's been ten long years since the boy went singing,
To his true love's door,
Crying 'Oh my true love, let me in'
Ten long years or more.

The great Galway traditional singer Seán Keane has recorded a lovely version of this song and sometimes sings it at his gigs. Sinéad Lohan used to do a beautiful version of it when she started out first. It's a song about first love. I have come across people singing it at sessions here and there. Recently I met a singer who told me that she always sings this song, '*Agus téann sé go smior ionam* – and it goes to the marrow in me,' she said.

The Stargazers

*A*fter I left my first band and walked away into the darkness, I left the rock band thing behind me and went acoustic. I wasn't great singing with the band really, it was too loud for me, and when I played the acoustic guitar I could sing much better. There used to be soccer matches in Cork at that time, the early 1980s, between the different bands. There were three teams – the Rockers, the Folkies and the Punks. I changed from being a Rocker to being a Folkie. I stopped hanging around Sir Henry's and started hanging around in the Phoenix Bar. There was very high-class traditional music played there that time. Jackie Daly, Séamus Creagh, Mick Daly, Colm Murphy, Matt Cranitch, Eoin Ó Riabhaigh, Henry Benagh, Jimmy Crowley – all great players. I loved traditional music, and I eventually learned the difference between a jig and a reel, a polka and a slide.

Cork was brilliant in the early 1980s: all those great trad heads; the inspired Jimmy MacCarthy; guitar maestro Declan

Sinnott; rock bands like Max Von Rap; punk bands like Nun Attax, Five Go Down To The Sea, Microdisney; folk bands like Stoker's Lodge and the Lee Valley String Band; great singers and performers like Mick the Punk and Mandy Murphy. Every year Rory Gallagher came and played a big gig around New Year. And we had a great place to hang out late at night called the Café Lorca – a literary café named for the Andalusian poet, full of writers, musicians, artists and head-the-balls. Jimmy Crowley used be there, and he gave me gigs playing bass with him. Jimmy is a great balladeer, song collector and scholar, and when I thought of it later, I realised that was a fantastic apprenticeship I got, playing with Jimmy Crowley, 'The Boys of Fairhill' himself. At the time I didn't fully appreciate that it was such an education, but it was, and I loved it. So I spent two summers doing gigs with Jimmy; we had Pat MacNamara from Tullagh, a brilliant musician, on the accordion, Johnny 'Fang' Murphy on guitar and me on bass. That was good work, and I was making proper money from playing music for the first time – fair play to Jimmy Crowley. Johnny Fang had a boat, a lovely Galway hooker, and we sometimes slept on the boat and sailed to the gigs down in west Cork, around Roaringwater Bay.

Johnny was at that time starting to move on his musical journey from folk to jazz, from Hank Williams to Jimmie Rodgers to Leon Redbone to Louis Armstrong. I had a great *grá* for fancy jazzy chords because of my Beatles education. I knew a lot of The Beatles' songs, which had sophisticated chord sequences – sixths and diminisheds, stuff like that. So Johnny and I started working out songs, and Johnny proposed getting in a third member and starting a band doing swingy, jazzy, old-fashioned material. We got in Chris Ahern, who was a really good acoustic player and who could play Django Reinhardt – gypsy stuff. We had great fun working out arrangements of classic old songs from the 1930s and 1940s by Irving Berlin, Cole Porter, Hoagy Carmichael, The Mills Brothers, The Ink Spots, The Andrews Sisters.

Johnny was on acoustic rhythm guitar and lead vocals, Chris played lead acoustic and the low harmonies, and I played electric bass and high harmonies. We used to be out in Johnny and Darby's house on the Lee Road practising two or three times a week, me and Chris at the oohs and aahs, me on the high harmony, Chris on the low, me walking the old bass up and down the fretboard, Johnny Fang chanting away like a champion. It was brilliant craic. And then Johnny came up with the name – The Stargazers. Perfect. We practised a lot for enjoyment before we ever thought of playing a gig. Then we did a few small gigs in a little room over O'Flynn's Bar on Union Quay. One night Johnny suggested we put on tuxedos and dicky bows for the gig. This was very funny – what a laugh. That became our gear and we went on to play together for about seven years. We were a fun and extremely tight band. We could nearly read each other's minds; if one fellah made a mistake, we would all nearly make it. They were great days, playing with The Stargazers. We played gigs all over Ireland, for a month in Portugal, once on the island of Bermuda and for two weeks in Zambia, Africa. We witnessed the perpetual rainbow at Victoria Falls and saw the hippos rising in the Zambezi river. One time we played in Kensington Roof Gardens, at the top of a very high London building, with flamingos and palm trees. Sometimes we played for the rich and sometimes we played for the craic. We played residencies in the Carmel Hotel in Kilkenny, the Metropole Hotel in Cork and the Harcourt Hotel in Dublin. We had great fun. It was lovely to be playing and hanging around with such sound blokes. It was good to meet up at Johnny's old brass workshop on Lavitts Quay, an Aladdin's cave of candlesticks and brass beds, load up the van and head off to an ol' gig up the country. I was very sorry to leave the band, but I was on the way to writing and singing my own songs, and never intended to spend seven years playing close-harmony swing jazz. Life is what happens when you're busy making other plans.

I Won't Be Afraid Any More

I won't be afraid of the window,
And I won't be afraid of the door,
Not even the wolves, hungry for blood,
Can worry me any more,
And because of your love,
I won't be afraid any more!

If I get lost in the city, start following people around,
If I lie down with the drunkards,
Or fall in the river and drown,
Because of your love,
I won't be afraid any more!

If I go rocking and rolling,
In pieces all over the floor,
If I meet death on the point of a blade,

I won't be afraid any more,
And because of your love,
I won't be afraid any more!

It's been a long time since I've seen you,
I might never see you again,
Some things are too good to be true,
And if I never see you again,
Still because of your love,
I won't be afraid any more!
I won't be afraid any more!

I had written a few good songs when I was in my early twenties, but then I had been stuck and suffered from writer's block for a good few years, only getting the odd song out. In 1994, I had reached the ripe old age of thirty-three and that was the year that the walls came tumbling down, and I finally got really going with the songwriting. 'I Won't Be Afraid Any More' was the big flagship number of this new fearless era. A lot of the positive approach I use in my writing now and in my writing workshops comes from this time.

One of the places that this song came from was a talk I heard the poet Nuala Ní Dhomhnaill give about protection poems in the Irish tradition. Oh, I could do with a few of those, I thought to myself, and then I bought a book called *Orthaí Cosanta sa Chráifeacht Cheilteach* (Protection Poems in the Celtic Faith). Saint Patrick's breastplate was there, and many other references to armour plating of various kinds. I spent £9 on that book. I saw that £9 as an investment that I was hoping to make back in the Hit Factory, and I did too. I took the line about meeting death on the point of a blade from one of my favourite Irish legends, *Suibhne Geilt* – Mad Sweeney, whose death at spearpoint was foretold because he clashed with the Church.

I would like to revisit this song sometime, with a big orchestra, massed choirs and maybe a band of angels, and really give it the full lash!

Nomos

When I left The Stargazers in 1992, I swore I wouldn't go joining any more bands and I was determined to start singing my own material, but I still didn't have all that many songs. I played in a duo for a while with Johnny McCarthy, a great musician who plays fiddle and flute. This was a halfway stage. It was half tunes and half songs. We played some lovely gigs in the Lobby Bar in Cork and had a few memorable jaunts, especially one trip to Blennerville in County Kerry. On a summer's night, we played in a pub with the local brass band, and Johnny blinded them all with his fiddle playing, while a woman danced a hornpipe in the middle of the floor. Some nights are full of magic. Who knows – maybe the moon was full, the tide was in, or the stars were lined up right. Maybe staying close to the music means you stay close to the magic.

Young traditional musicians of a very high standard were flocking to Cork at that time from all around Ireland, England and other places because of the rich musical heritage left in

University College Cork by Seán Ó Riada, Aloys Fleischmann and Tomás Ó Canainn, and because the great Mícheál Ó Súilleabháin, an inspiring and charismatic musician, was head of music there. I walked into the Spailpín Fánach pub one evening to witness an incredible session of traditional music. There were players like Niall Vallelly, Liz Doherty, Niall Keegan, Brendan Ring, Frank Torpey and Gerry McKee lashing out a new, crazily energetic form of Irish music. It was a shock to the senses. It was mad. They obviously had no respect for any of the conservative or staid elements of the music. I loved it. It seemed to me to be far more rock and roll than rock and roll itself. Some of the punters used to be giving out that they played way too fast. One night I brought along an amp and my fretless electric bass. That drove them clean mad altogether, and it seemed to drive the session to even crazier, dizzying heights.

Nomos was a brilliant young traditional band that I joined in the summer of 1992. Even though I'd sworn I wouldn't go joining another band when I left The Stargazers, I went and joined another band. This was a very different style of music, though. This was lightning fast, wild trad music. 'I Won't Be Afraid Any More' was the title track of the first Nomos album, which was released in Ireland in 1995 and in the US the following year. I remember when we were recording it in 1994, *Riverdance* came on TV, which was very exciting. There was a huge set-dancing craze in Ireland at that time, too. The brilliant Begley and Cooney were the main attraction. TG4 launched in 1996. It seemed to be a time of a big resurgence in Irish culture. *I Won't Be Afraid Any More* was our particular version of it, like.

The first Nomos members were Niall Vallelly on concertina, Liz Doherty on fiddle, Frank Torpey on bodhrán (actually a Moroccan bendir) and Gerry McKee on mandocello. Then I joined on guitar, electric fretless bass and songs. After the first album, Liz left and Vince Milne came in on fiddle. We toured extensively for a few years: America, Canada, Germany, Scandinavia, Britain, France. It was an exciting time, and an energising experience for me. I was saturating myself deep in Irish music. We were a high energy, full on, rockin' band, and we lifted the roof off many a venue.

We released a second album, *Set You Free*, in 1997. I left the band shortly after that to launch my solo career, and Eoin Coughlan came in as the singer and bassist. All that touring was fun, but I was away from home too much and missing my people. A lot of the great Irish traditional bands, such as Altan, Lúnasa, The Chieftains, Danú and Beoga, spend an awful lot of time on the road, and the attraction can wear off fairly quickly. It is a great way to see the world, but in the end there's no place like home, and as many musicians will tell you, the cup of tea at home in your own kitchen is the best part of any tour.

All The Ways You Wander

All the ways you wander, all the ways you roam,
All across great oceans, all across the foam,
Through the faraway houses, through the sunsets on fire,
Searching for the island of your heart's desire.

Where the sun is always shining, and the oranges grow
    on the trees,
You only have to wait two seconds there, for everything
    you please,
In a garden of daisies, in a circle of light,
Searching for the island, of your heart's delight.

I'll wait for you, like a true friend,
I'll wait for you, till the very end.

And if you take the long way, if you take the long way home,
Down where the magicians and the dreamers roam,

Through the mountains of morning, through the valleys
  of night,
Searching for the island of your heart's delight.

I'll wait for you, like a true friend,
I'll wait for you, till the very end.

This is my favourite of all the songs I've written – so far, like. I
wrote this song for my daughter Leslie. I started it when she was
two and I finished it when she was six. There she was, one lovely
summer's day, out the back, splashing around in a little paddling
pool, and the sun streaming down. My heart filled with love for
her. I tried to describe this feeling in a song and this is what I
got. When I came across this melody on my guitar I was sure it
must have been another song already – it sounded so familiar. I
asked everyone I knew if they could identify it and no one could,
so I figured in the end that I must have composed it myself. I
like to think that there are all these melodies floating around in
the air – all we have to do is catch one and pull it down to earth.
Leslie moved to Spain with her mum just before her sixth
birthday, and that was the time I finished the song.

I've recorded this loads of times, but my favourite version is
the first one, with the group Nomos. It was on the first Nomos
album, *I Won't Be Afraid Any More*, with the great maestro
Mícheál Ó Súilleabháin on piano. Pauline Scanlon, the lovely
singer from Dingle, does a beautiful version of this song. Many
people around Ireland and abroad have sung it at sing-songs and
traditional sessions, at weddings and funerals. I love that.

A lot of people tell me it is my best song, but gentle reader,
you ain't seen nothing yet!

PART TWO

Everything's Turning to Gold, Cathy

Everything's Turning to Gold, Cathy

Everything's turning to gold, Cathy,
And the sun is setting in the islands,
Above the town there's two swans flying,
Away home to heaven.

And many's the heart was broken,
Many the weary traveller,
Couldn't even have imagined,
Such a heaven.

And who are we to go golden,
Through the streets, through the islands,
Through the long days dying,
Through the shadows?

And who are we to go laughing and smiling?
Who are we to go hoping and dreaming?
Who are we to go walking like children home?

Everything's turning to gold, Cathy,
Everything old and worn,
Everything tired and torn,
From the journey.

And who are we to go golden?
Through the field, through the forest,
Through the night, through the harvest,
Through the shadows?

And who are we to go laughing and smiling?
Who are we to go hoping and dreaming?
Who are we to go walking like children home?

Everything's turning to gold, Cathy,
And the sun is setting in the islands,
Above the town there's two swans flying,
Away home to heaven.

I met Cathy in August 1994 and I wrote this song only about six weeks into our relationship. It was a big leap. If she broke it off with me then I would be left with my best song, and no Cathy! It was October and the leaves were turning to a beautiful gold, and so were we. I bravely sang her the song and she cried.

I suppose you could say the two swans are a bit like the two swans in the Irish legend *The Wooing of Etain*, in which two lovers are transformed into swans and escape through the roof of Tara.

My old friend Noel Brazil, a brilliant songwriter who died in 2001, loved this song. 'You have got one song into the Pantheon, John,' he used to tell me. He meant the Pantheon of Great Songs!

I have often shied away from doing this song at gigs because it is so personal, and also because sometimes you can sing a song too much, and ruin it, and I don't want this one ever to get ruined on me.

We're Going Sailing

We're going sailing, out on the silver sea,
The air is full of treasure, you and me.
All along the shore you can hear the mermaids singing,
'No one will believe us, no one will believe us!'
And below on the strand, the sea is answering the land,
'No one will believe us!'

We're going sailing, for three nights and three days,
There are one hundred islands, in Roaringwater Bay.
There on the hill, the good people are living still,
'No one will believe us, no one will believe us!'
And we'll wake in the dawn, in the shadow of the thorn,
'No one will believe us!'

How high is the mountain, how deep is the sea,
How wide is the ocean, between you and me,

Underneath the waves, dolphins play the same games,
'No one will believe us, no one will believe us!'
And we'll wake in the dawn, in the shadow of the thorn,
'No one will believe us!'

Where did we get the money, how did we live so long?
To be out on the ocean, to be singing this song?
All along the shore you can hear the mermaids singing,
'No one will believe us, no one will believe us!'
And below on the strand, the sea is answering the land,
'No one will believe us!'

We're going sailing out on the silver sea,
The air is full of treasure, you and me.

Hey lads, I wasn't really going sailing like, I was just trying to describe a feeling. I mean there was no boat, no sea or strand, just this really good feeling of having come around a corner into a brighter, bigger, better place. So all the images in the song are just metaphors, gentle reader. Also, I wasn't talking to anyone in particular, just expressing a vague feeling of 'HERE WE GO!'

The feeling was right, too. Many good things happened after I wrote this song. I was lucky enough to get a really good manager, Lorcan Ennis of Verge Management. The first time Lorcan rang me up, I swear, I knew some really good things were going to happen. And they did.

Lorcan got me signed! Just before my fortieth birthday, when I had been playing in bands, doing all kinds of solo gigs and writing songs for maybe twenty years, I got discovered and signed a contract with the greatest record company in the world, EMI Records. Wow, EMI! Same label as the Beatles! I'd often noticed that EMI logo on the sleeves of many great records when I was a kid lying on the floor, listening to the record player.

'We're Going Sailing' was my first single on the EMI label. There is a most beautiful animation of it made by Frank Prendergast of 9mm Film, which you can watch on YouTube. It was a sign of brighter days to come. Myself and Lorcan have been working away successfully together now for some sixteen years, and the best is yet to come, gentle reader – watch this space!

It Wasn't to Be

It wasn't to be, or we'd be walking in the same room,
It wasn't to be, or we'd be standing the same ground,
It wasn't to be, or we'd be drinking from the wells of
the world,
Or living in each other's shadow.

The same sun, the same sun that rises on you,
Leaves me here in sorrow,
The same sun in the sky that smiles on you,
Smiles on me tomorrow.

It wasn't to be, or you'd be standing next to me,
It wasn't to be, you could wish for nothing finer,
It wasn't to be, or we'd be drinking from the wells of
the world,
Or living in each other's shadow.

And would we go, would we go together, love,
Or would we go away down alone,
Would we go climbing the rocks by the seashore,
Or follow one another home?

What will we do with our houses and our lands, love?
What will we do with our dreams and our towers?
Lay them bare to the birds of the air,
And go far from one another.

It wasn't to be, or we'd be walking in the same room,
It wasn't to be, or we'd be standing the same ground,
It wasn't to be, or we'd be drinking from the wells of
    the world,
Or living in each other's shadow.

I invented a new style of music called '*sean-nós* blues'. It was a fusion of Gaelic traditional singing and African rock-and-roll blues. 'It Wasn't to Be' is in this style. There's only one chord in it: D. So, I got my big rhythm going, and my one chord, and I'm lamenting away. I borrowed some imagery from a traditional folk song called 'What Put the Blood' for the last verse. I heard that song from Paddy Tunney, a singer from Fermanagh. I used to go to the Cork City Music Library for years to get out albums and cassettes of traditional folk songs. I used to do a great version of 'It Wasn't to Be' when it was new, with Mick Daly and Áine Whelan on harmonies.

When I wrote this song, my relationship had ended and I was very down. I found great healing in music and songwriting. I wrote a load of sad songs. I used to worry that the songs were so sad, but now I think that if I could go back there, I would write even more sad songs, because things change and the sadness passes away, and then you can't write such sad songs any more, and sad songs are a beautiful thing.

Not too Bad

Yeera Yeah, Yeerah Yeah, Not Too Bad.

Feelings My Eye walked into the bar, said
'Not a Tall Boy – there you are!'
Not a Tall Boy was talking to someone new,
Not a Tall reckoned you'd do, and you do.

Not Too Bad, Not Too Bad, Yeerah Yeah, Not Too Bad.

The Boys at the Back were Having the Crack,
And Hopping the Ball to you,
You Didn't Flinch or Give Them an Inch, did you?
One of Them dribbled 'You'll do', and you do.

Not Too Bad, Not Too Bad, Yeerah Yeah, Not Too Bad.

Not Too Bad, that's how I am Not Too Bad,
Don't talk about happy or sad, say 'Not Too Bad',

Don't Tell Anyone what you're thinking,
They'll think that you're mad,
Say 'Not Too Bad, Not Too Bad.'

Yeera Yeah, Yeerah Yeah, Not Too Bad!

For most of my twenties I wrote hardly any songs but I sometimes wrote down lyrics in an old copybook. When I got going later on, I revisited that copybook and got this song out of it. The song is set in the Phoenix Bar in Cork and I made up characters like 'Feelings My Eye', 'Not Too Bad' and 'Not a Tall Boy'. These are cynical, dark people who put you down and keep you in your place. 'Not Too Bad' is as good as it gets in the photographic negative of this song. Declan Sinnott really got into this song and did a great arrangement of it on the *Wells of the World* album. He called it 'a great attack on mediocrity'.

When You and I Were True

Oh we might as well lie down, love,
Lie down and close our eyes,
We might as well go walking,
In the country of the blind,
The long grass has grown,
The wild birds flown,
To their homes away in the blue,
And nothing's left the same,
The whole world's changed,
Since you and I were true.

Oh and how can a story be ended,
When it didn't hardly begin,
How can my glass be so empty,
When it's filled up to the brim,
And it wasn't always so,

It wasn't always so,
We had something better to do,
And it didn't always rain,
Every single day,
When you and I were true.

In the country where we're heading, love,
There is nothing but rocks and stones,
No friendly plant or animal,
No angel to guide you home,
Until the day you'll find,
In the country of the blind,
Some wanderer just like you,
And the singing of a bird,
Nobody has heard,
Since you and I were true.

On my eighteenth birthday I got a full-time permanent and pensionable job in Bank of Ireland, and two years later I left it to become a full-time professional musician. My mother nearly killed me. 'If you leave your good job in the bank,' says she, 'don't ever come back to this house again!' Then when I rang her and told her I had handed in my notice, she said, 'Ah sure, we'll see you Friday night.'

On my way to being a successful musician, I gave a lot of guitar lessons. I considered this part of the work. I had a guitar in my hand the whole time so I was honing my skills at the same time as teaching. I taught half of Cork how to play the guitar. This led to work with community youth groups. I taught rock and roll to kids in Mahon who were in trouble with the law, in the crying room at the back of the church. Then I got a job two days a week teaching music in Cork Prison. It was my old buddy Noel Shine got me that. Noel has done great work for years teaching music in that lonesome prison up on Rathmore Road. Then I also taught in Spike Island Prison for about five years. That was an education. I met many incredible people with extraordinary stories. There was something incredibly sad about certain songs you'd hear the prisoners singing. I remember this guy doing time for murder singing:

> Listen to the rhythm of the falling rain,
> Tellin' me what a fool I've been.

It would break your heart to listen to that.

I wrote 'When You and I Were True' in the music classroom in Cork Prison, after work, when there was nobody around. It was just getting dark outside the bars of the window, and it was raining. There was a terrible air of sadness all around. The song is made up of bits and pieces of lines I had before, from songs that were never finished. The chord sequence is the same as 'No Woman No Cry' or 'Let It Be'. The tune is very like a traditional song from the north called '*Airdí Cuan*', a lament, or '*Siúil a Rún*', which is similar.

The song has a few names: 'When You and I Were True', 'Since You and I Were True' and I've seen it called 'If You and I Were True'. One of the first times I sang it, I was heard by a singer called Méav Ní Mhaolchatha, who made advances through Colm Ó Snodaigh of Kíla to ask me for the song. I sent it along, with pride, from my Hit Factory. Next thing, Méav comes out with this to-die-for version of my song, and then she goes on to become a star with the million-selling *Celtic Woman*. It's so nice to hear someone with a beautiful voice singing one of your songs. It's like a dream. Pauline Scanlon, another clear, angelic, bright and wonderful voice, has also recorded a version.

The terrible air of sadness has stayed in the song, and sometimes you can lay a room low with the desolation.

I'm Going to Set You Free

If you did, if you did,
Even if you did,
Been where you shouldn't have been,
Seen what you shouldn't have seen,
Dreamed what you shouldn't have dreamed,
That doesn't mean you have to be locked up here forever,
I'm going to set you free!

And if you did, if you did,
Even if you did,
Done what you shouldn't have done,
Run when you shouldn't have run,
Lost when you should have won,
That doesn't mean you have to be locked up here forever,
I'm going to set you free!

If you did, if you did,
Even if you did,
Strayed from the beaten track,
Maybe you never got back,
Went in off the black,
That doesn't mean you have to be paying the price forever,
I'm going to set you free!

If you did, if you did,
Even if you did,
Suffered from a broken heart,
Got off to a poor start,
Maybe you fell apart.
That doesn't mean you have to be paying the price forever,
I'm going to set you free!

And if you did, if you did,
Ah you know you did,
Known what you shouldn't have known,
Shown what you shouldn't have shown,
Thrown what you shouldn't have thrown,
That doesn't mean you have to be lying round here forever,
I'm going to set you free!
I'm going to set you free!

Well there I was, lads, like the old song says, just going down the road feeling bad, when I felt a light being turned on inside me and I just started making up the song. It turned out to be the title track of the second Nomos album, and it has been covered by The Battlefield Band, Shooglenifty and The Outside Track. The Scots like it, like.

'I'm going to set you free,' I said to myself, as I was walking down George's Quay in Cork, singing away, and so I made up my mind to set myself free of the past and to have a good go off the future. Like the Irish proverb: *Is fearr súil romhainn ná dhá shúil inár ndiaidh* – it's better to have one eye ahead of us than two eyes behind us.

Meet Me on the Midnight Shore

*Meet me on the midnight shore, meet me on the
  midnight shore,*
*Meet me on the midnight shore, meet me on the
  midnight shore,*

How are ya gonna break a heart that has been broken
  before?
*Meet me on the midnight shore, meet me on the
  midnight shore,*

Has been broken before, and can be broken some more,
*Meet me on the midnight shore, meet me on the
  midnight shore,*

Now we know that this world is burning, and there's a
fire at the heart's core,

Meet me on the midnight shore, meet me on the
midnight shore,

For tonight I'm gonna take you sailing, to the island of
the strong door,
Meet me on the midnight shore, meet me on the
midnight shore,

There I'll shut your wild, wild eyes, with kisses four,
Meet me on the midnight shore, meet me on the
midnight shore,

Moondrum, moondrum, beating on the ocean floor,
Meet me on the midnight shore, meet me on the
midnight shore,

Now we know that this world is burning, and there's a
fire at the heart's core,
Meet me on the midnight shore, meet me on the
midnight shore.

I tried for a while to write a song a month. This is a good trick, because you can train yourself to do it, and then you feel the space opening up the next month in which you are waiting for the next song to appear. My daughter got a better piano at that time; I had her old banger of a piano in the back room and I just made up this song on it, not knowing what I was talking about really. I found myself borrowing a few lines from a poem I had learned at school by John Keats called 'La Belle Dame Sans Merci'. Thank you, John Keats. And I made up a new English word: 'moondrum'!

Brian Kennedy came and sang backing vocals on the recording, produced by Declan Sinnott, that we made in Sun Studios in Temple Bar, Dublin, for the album *Will We Be Brilliant or What?*

The Poor Weary Wanderer

My heart goes out to you,
Poor weary wanderer,
Forced to travel this world alone,
Forced to wander away from home.

You must sow what you cannot reap,
You must hold what you cannot keep,
You must fear what you cannot know,
You must feel what you cannot speak.

Nobody wants you,
Nobody needs you,
Nobody cares for you,
Nobody slaves for you.

You can't see the angels,
Gather all around you,

You can't hear what they're saying,
In heaven all about you.

My heart goes out to you,
Poor weary wanderer,
Forced to travel this world alone,
Forced to wander away from home.

My heart goes out to you,
Poor weary wanderer,
You must lie in the cold clay,
You must travel to the end of day.

It was a fine summer's day and I decided to head off on my bike, out to the river. I went to the Lee Fields for a swim and got in above the weir. I've been swimming in the Lee since I was a boy. I dived in and splashed around. When I came out, there was this old man sitting there next to me on a bench. I asked him if he knew what time it was; I was thinking of heading home, like. Well, he looked at me and in the saddest, weariest voice I have ever heard in my life, he told me that it was six o'clock. The way he said 'six o'clock' was absolutely tragic! The poor man, God knows what he was going through. I wrote this song about him on the way home. I never saw him there again, this poor weary wanderer.

I have a story about the tune as well. It goes like this: I was sharing a flat at that time with Ger Wolfe, a fantastic poetic, songwriter and lovely fellah. We were living in a grand spot across the road from St Finbarr's Cathedral, and every Sunday morning and Wednesday evening they would ring the bells. The bells were really loud and would completely fill the flat with their music.

The bell ringers weren't the greatest musicians you ever heard, and they mostly just played the scale, descending – do ti la so fa mi re do – over and over. And over. I don't think they ever really got the hang of it. The funny thing about it was, after a few months you would get so used to it that you would not hear it any more. It was after about six months of this that a pattern began to creep into both my and Ger's songs: the descending scale. The tune of 'The Poor Weary Wanderer' is simply the sound of the bells, falling, falling, over and over again.

Róisín Elsafty, a brilliant *sean nós* singer from Bearna in Connemara, did a really excellent version of this on her album *Má Bhíonn Tú Liom Bí Liom*, produced by Dónal Lunny. This is nearly my favourite version of one of my songs by other people – except, of course, for Christy Moore. The craic with Christy beats all, like.

A Songwriting Workshop.
Right Now!

Gentle reader, there are many ways to write a song, but I am just going to use one of them here for this workshop. It's called 'the fast song', written in under half an hour. The first thing you do is cut off all negative thoughts. You are not allowed to attack your work in any way during the workshop. In fact, you must do the opposite: you must shower it with praise, build it up, feed it with positive energy and allow it to grow, blossom and bloom. You must feed it with love and Miracle-Gro.

There are a few parts to the workshop:

1. Decide what you are going to write about. Give yourself perhaps one or two minutes to do this; if you like, you can take more time, perhaps two or three minutes, but it's better if you pick something straight away. Go for it.

2. Write like mad for about five minutes. Write down anything that comes into your head about your chosen subject – stream of consciousness, like: words, phrases,

sentences, anything. Don't worry about rhyming, don't worry about anything, just write away like billy-o.

3. Pick out the few best bits of what you've written, and they're the lyrics of your song. Now you apply the 'tricks of the trade': a bit of rhyming, lots of repetition, a few oohs and aahs, or whack-fol-de-diddles, or whatever you're having yourself.

4. Sing it. The first thing that comes into your head, that's your song. Open up your gob and sing the words out. Making up the melody is like coming to the edge of a cliff, and just jumping off and flying. Singing, like. You can't get hurt. It's an imaginary cliff.

5. Defend your song. Don't attack it. For God's sake, it's only an ol' biteen of a song, like. Build it up. Improve it. Sing it.

Sounds easy, and it is. Because we don't really know what we are doing when we write a song, do we? We are just blending words and musical notes, and we hit on lovely things by accident. You can try this at home. Knock yourself out. It really works! What is music, anyway, reader, only a magical, invisible, untouchable material that we don't really understand at all, but that means so much to us? Music is therapeutic, relaxing, engaging. It takes you away on journeys through the air. It is beautiful stuff, this music. It floats around you like a magical substance, intangible, unassailable; it has no scent or any real substance. It is wonderful. It is always a pleasure to make music, to command these magic notes to rise and fall. Hey, I think I'll make a song out of that!

Will we be brilliant or what, gentle reader? Brilliant or *what*?

PART THREE

Will We Be All Dressed in Sunlight?

Will We Be Brilliant or What?

What's in this world?
What have you seen happening here?
Here in this world,
What have you been doing here?
What's on your mind, what's in your heart?
What have you got?

And will we be brilliant or what?
Will we be all dressed in sunlight?
Brilliant or what?
Will we be smiling under starlight?
Brilliant or what?
Will we be graceful and free, will we be?
Graceful and free?
Radiant and glorious, why not?
What have you got?
Will we be brilliant, brilliant or what?

Born to be bright, to be near sunlight
Born to be warm, to be safe from harm
Make up your mind, take up your time
Ready or not.

Will we be brilliant or what?
Will we be all dressed in sunlight?
Brilliant or what?
Will we be smiling under starlight?
Brilliant or what?
Will we be graceful and free, will we be?
Graceful and free?
Will we be kind? Why not,
What have you got?
And will we be brilliant or what?
Brilliant or what?

When living to be living – *Will we be brilliant or what?*
When loving to be loving – *Will we be brilliant or what?*
When learning to be learning – *Will we be brilliant or*
    what?
When laughing to be laughing – *Will we be brilliant or*
    what?
When leaving to be leaving – *Will we be brilliant or*
    what?
When living to be living – *Will we be brilliant or what?*
When loving to be loving – *Will we be brilliant or what?*
When learning to be learning – *Will we be brilliant or*
    what?

The first line of this song is something that was said to me by Peadar Ó Riada from Coolea. Peadar is a brilliant musician and composer, and has run the amazing Cór Chúil Aodha (The Coolea Choir) ever since his father Seán died in 1971. Peadar was very kind to me and always spoke to me in Irish. One night when we were sitting in the kitchen in Coolea, he opened up a philosophical discussion by asking me, in Irish, this big question: 'What's in this world?' Anything big like that that's asked of you, you are not going to forget, and that phrase stayed with me for years until I put it into this song. *Go raibh maith agat, a Pheadair!*

Will We Be Brilliant Or What? became the title of my first album with EMI Records in 2002. It caught on and became a kind of slogan. People got a great kick out of it, like, and they smile when they say it. It's an anthem of positivity. I was joined by Juliet Turner from County Tyrone on the recording. Juliet is an excellent musician, and one of the new breed of Irish singers who sing in their own accents. This is what I call 'the accent wars'. You have The Saw Doctors from Tuam, Christy Moore from Kildare, Damien Dempsey from Dublin, Juliet from Tyrone and myself, all singing in our own glorious regional accents – as opposed to those who sing in phoney American accents, like. Fair play to us!

Magic Nights in the Lobby Bar

(Words: John Spillane, Ricky Lynch, Ger Wolfe.
Music: John Spillane)

They were magic nights in the Lobby Bar,
With Brendan Ring playing Madame Bonaparte,
And every note the piper would play,
Would send me away, send me away,
Away through the window, away through the rain,
Away 'cross the city, away in the air,
To a field by a river, where the trees are so green,
The deepest of green you've ever seen,
Where once you have been, you can go back again,
You can go any time, you can go any time,
'Cos it's only in your mind.

They were magic nights in the Lobby Bar,
With Ricky Lynch and his golden guitar, singing:

'Autumn in Mayfield and the barley was ripe,
The harvest moon hung low in the sky,
We were children and our mothers were young
And fathers were tall and kind.'

And every word that Ricky would play,
Would send me away, send me away,
Away through the window, away through the rain,
Away 'cross the city, away in the air,
To a field by a river, where the trees are so green,
The deepest of green you've ever seen,
Where once you have been, you can go back again,
You can go any time, you can go any time,
'Cos it's only in your mind.

They were magic nights in the Lobby Bar,
When Ger Wolfe would sing like a lark, singing:
'Winter hung her coat on a hanger of dark'
And *'I am the blood of Erin, spilt in an empty cave,*
I am the flower of Ireland, out on the drifting wave,
I am the lark of Mayfield, tumbling down the hill,
I am the child of summer, I can remember you still.'

And every word that Ger would say,
Would send me away, send me away,
Away through the window, away through the rain,
On a carriage of music, away in the air,
To a field by a river, where the trees are so green,
The deepest of green that you've ever seen,

Where once you have been, you can go back again,
You can go any time, you can go any time,
'Cos it's only in your mind.

'It was Autumn in Mayfield and the barley was ripe,
The harvest moon hung low in the sky,
We were children and our mothers were young
And fathers were tall and kind.'

I am very proud of this song. The Lobby Bar was a wonderful music venue in Cork city and the owner Pat Conway was a brilliant promoter and supporter of music. Monica McNamara wrote a book about all the great music that went on there called *The Lobby Bar*. I played many, many gigs in the Lobby: solo gigs, gigs as John Spillane and Johnny McCarthy, The Stargazers, John Spillane and Declan Sinnott, John Spillane and Sinéad Lohan, Nomos, John Spillane and Ger Wolfe, The Curly Lambs, etc. When the Lobby closed its doors in 2005, I had played more gigs there than anyone else.

I had many magical musical experiences in the Lobby, and I picked three of them for the three verses of this song. Some of the most beautiful lines are from Ricky Lynch's song 'Autumn in Mayfield' and from Ger Wolfe's song 'The Lark of Mayfield'. This device I call the 'song within the song'. I got this idea from William Shakespeare, who sometimes used the device of the 'play within the play'. I had no idea that the Lobby was going to close when I wrote this song, and I am so glad now that I was able to give something back to Pat, and to capture some of those memories.

The Dance of the Cherry Trees

Let me tell you 'bout the cherry trees,
Every April in our town,
They put on the most outrageous clothes,
And they sing and they dance around.

Hardly anybody sings or dances,
Hardly anybody dances or sings,
In this town that I call my own,
You have to hand it to the cherry trees.

And they seem to be saying,
To me anyway,
'You know we've travelled all around the sun,
You know it's taken us one whole year,
Well done everyone, well done!
On behalf of me and the cherry trees,
Well done!'

Cherry blossom in the air,
Cherry blossom on the street,
Cherry blossom in your hair,
And a blossom at your feet.

You know we've travelled all around the sun,
You know it's taken us one whole year,
Well done everyone, well done!
On behalf of me and the cherry trees,
Well done!

You know me, sometimes I think I'm getting old,
Not as young as I used to be,
So it means even more to me,
To see the dance of the cherry trees,
And they seem to be saying,
Is it only to me?

'You know we've travelled all around the sun,
You know it's taken us one whole year,
Well done everyone, well done!
On behalf of me and the cherry trees,
Well done!'

The flowering of the cherry blossoms in the spring brings this song back every year. Released in 2002 on the *Will We Be Brilliant Or What?* album, it seems to grow in popularity every year. In 2011, it was played on the six o'clock news. Long may it continue.

Many people like this song for its positivity. I was feeling very low and run down when I wrote it. It was Easter weekend 1998, the third week of April; the weather was cold, grey and miserable. I was broke and I had no gigs for Easter. I was also recovering from an illness called a spontaneous pneumothorax, or a collapsed lung.

My side felt so sore I thought something might have been wrong and I made my way to the A & E department in the Regional Hospital, where I was left waiting and got forgotten about! Eventually I figured I wasn't too bad and I wandered off, feeling miserable. The first cherry tree I met was at the Wilton roundabout. In full bloom, it seemed to shine with an unearthly beauty in the midst of the doom and grey gloom. I then got the bus home to Passage West and became aware of every cherry tree I passed along the way. There are some gorgeous big ones on the way into Passage, around the bust of Father O'Flynn, but the one in the middle of the square beats all. Growing out of the concrete, its roots have spread magnificently, and its long arms scatter their blossoms freely all around the town. I got home and sat down and wrote the song. At first it was a much slower and sadder song, but as I got into better form myself, the song cheered up as well.

There is a road called Pearse Road in Ballyphehane in Cork, which is lined with cherry trees and is well worth a visit in April. It's also interesting to travel up through Ireland in the cherry blossom season and see how they open first in the south and about seven to ten days later in the far north.

These trees come from Japan, and this is the song that brought me to Japan! Yoko and Keiko of the Music Plant, Tokyo, invited me there in 2003, where I played about ten gigs in seven days all over Japan. I was travelling with, and opening for, my friends in the great Irish traditional band Lúnasa. We landed in Hiroshima, City of Peace, city of trees, just as the blossoms were in full swing. We were taken straight to the museum of the genocide that was the atomic bomb, and that was a harrowing experience. Hiroshima is now all about healing and peace, and many cities around the world have given it presents of seeds and trees.

The writing of 'The Dance of the Cherry Trees' on that grey Cork afternoon was to bring me on a journey that continues from year to year as these lovely trees burst back into flower every April. April 2016 saw me performing a new arrangement of the song by Eva MacMullan and Padraig Wallace with the great UCC Choir on RTÉ's *The Late Late Show*. Happy days in the Hit Factory!

Let the River Flow

You lost your key, and you can't go home,
Take a walk around town, be on your own,
And your feet are drawn down to the riverside,
You sit on the stone, and you talk to the tide.

Let the river go, let the river go, let the river go,
Where the river must go, let the river flow.

And you never know who you might meet,
When you come to the corner, and you cross the street,
And you walk in the door of Charlie's Bar,
And you look at the world through the empty jar.

Let the river go, let the river go, let the river go,
Where the river must go, let the river flow.

Ah, here comes Séamus, with his boyish grin,
And his crazy poems, you always like to see him,
But you wish that he didn't have to feel such pain,
Such pain that he doesn't know if he's going or he's
     staying.

Let the river go, let the river go, let the river go,
Where the river must go, let the river flow.

And here's Fionbarra, with his coat and his hood,
Lovely fellah, not lookin' too good,
And you wish that he didn't have to feel such pain,
Such pain that he doesn't know if he's going or he's
     staying.

Let the river go, let the river go, let the river go,
Where the river must go, let the river flow.

If the world was an apple, if the world was a pear,
If the world was a cherry, still it wouldn't be fair.

Let the river go, let the river go, let the river go,
Where the river must go, let the river flow.

My old friend Larry Roddy used to say that this was my best
song. He considered it a perfect song, he used to say. At the time
I had it first, around 2001, he was invited onto RTÉ Radio One
to play his favourite five songs and 'Let the River Flow' was one
of them. That was a great compliment coming from Larry, a man
who loved music and who loved the blues. Larry was a music

agent and a lovely man. He booked me gigs and kept me going when I was let down by other people. He had a secret Ireland, a network of little acoustic venues north and south of the border: Magherafelt, Ramelton, Carrick-on-Shannon, Ballymore Eustace. He passed away in 2010, and is fondly remembered by many of us in music.

This song was written in great sadness when two people I knew had a hand in their own deaths. May they rest in peace.

The Madwoman of Cork

(Words: Patrick Galvin. Music: John Spillane)

Today
Is the feast day of Saint Anne.
Pray for me,
I am the madwoman of Cork.

Yesterday
In Castle Street
I saw two goblins at my feet,
I saw a horse without a head
Carrying the dead
To the graveyard
Near Turner's Cross.

I am the madwoman of Cork
No one talks to me.

When I walk in the rain
The children throw stones at me,
Old men persecute me
And women close their doors.
When I die,
Believe me,
They'll set me on fire.

I am the madwoman of Cork,
I have no sense.

Sometimes,
With an eagle in my brain,
I can see a train
Crashing at the station.
If I told people that
They'd choke me.
Then where would I be?

I am the madwoman of Cork
The people hate me.

When Canon Murphy died
I wept on his grave.
That was twenty-five years ago.
When I saw him just now
In Dunbar Street,
He had clay in his teeth.
He blest me.

I am the madwoman of Cork,
The clergy pity me.

I see death
In the branches of a tree,
Birth in the feathers of a bird.
To see a child with one eye
Or a woman buried in ice
Is the worst thing
And cannot be imagined.

I am the madwoman of Cork,
My mind fills me.

I should like to be young,
To dress up in silk
And have nine children.
I'd like to have red lips
But I'm eighty years old.
I have nothing
But a small house with no windows.

I am the madwoman of Cork,
Go away from me.

And if I die now,
Don't touch me.
I want to sail in a long boat
From here to Roche's Point
And there I will anoint

The sea
With oil of alabaster.

I am the madwoman of Cork
And today
Is the feast day of Saint Anne.
Feed me.

What a brilliant writer, Patrick Galvin. Born in Cork in 1927, he wrote many great poems, songs, stories and plays. My favourite Irish poet, he is still not that well known, even though he was far more brilliant than some poets that are well known. I was never aware of him, growing up in Cork. Nobody told me about him. The first I heard of him was a song he wrote called 'James Connolly'. 'Where, oh where is our James Connolly?' It's great to hear Damien Dempsey singing it now, and before that, Andy Irvine. Christy Moore sang it on the classic *Prosperous* album. What a song. 'Who will carry the burning flag?'

Patrick lived in Belfast, writing plays, for many years, and then he moved back to Cork with his wife Mary and family in the 1980s. I saw himself and Séamus Creagh, the great fiddler, playing in the Lobby Bar around 1993: poems, stories and tunes. It was my first time seeing him. I went up to him and I said, 'You're the best of the whole lot of them.' *Song for a Poor Boy*, his autobiography up to the age of twelve, is his prose masterpiece. The follow-up, *Song for a Raggy Boy*, was made into a famous film. But the poems! They beat all. I had learned 'The Madwoman of Cork' off by heart for pleasure, and though I tried a few times to put music to it, it wasn't until after Paddy had a stroke and was laid low, and that I was upset, like, that I rose up and lashed out the music to make it into a song.

Paddy was sound. He had no need for airs or graces, or superiority. He and Mary set up the Munster Literature Centre, and I did a fair few gigs for him and with him there. He and Mary provided great support and encouragement to struggling writers, myself included. I loved him. When I was doing my radio show on Raidió na Gaeltachta, Paddy turned eighty. He was in a wheelchair after the stroke, and I did a full two-hour tribute to him. I went behind his back to Mary and got a suss on his favourite songs and poems of all time: Gaelic, Spanish, South American, etc. I did a good job of it.

Patrick Galvin died in 2011, and we gave him a mighty send-off. Michael D. Higgins, later President of Ireland, read one of Paddy's poems over the coffin in Rocky Island Crematorium in Cork Harbour, and I was given the great honour of singing the poet down into the flames – 'When I die, believe me, they'll set me on fire.' Reader, they were lovely people, Paddy Galvin and Mary Johnson; 'His arms were summer round her waist.' There was a lot of love there, and I don't care, think what you like, but I'm going to put it into this book now, gentle reader, what Mary sent me:

Dearest John,

Thank you so much for expressing your love for Paddy so magnificently and for giving him such a send-off. He got great joy listening over and over to the radio program you dedicated to him at eighty. That said it all. You are one in a million. Hope to see you soon.

Love,
Mary and on behalf of Grainne and Macdara

Mary Johnson, Patrick's wife, cared for him lovingly during the last years of his life, and put together a lovely send-off, but what we didn't know and what she didn't say was that Mary herself was suffering from cancer at that time, and she passed away five months after Paddy. May they rest in peace. I'll say it again – who's going to stop me in my own book, like? – what a brilliant writer. Patrick Galvin. His selected poems are available from Cork University Press.

So who was she, the Madwoman of Cork? It doesn't matter because all the old people are gone now, as you and I will be gone too, lovely reader, any moment now. Paddy told me he wrote it about a woman who used to be over around Green Street in the 1950s. When I was small, in the 1960s, there was a woman we called Nan Bird who used to wander around Cork. She was mad. Dressed in black, terrifying looking, all bent over, like a witch, one hand behind her back always – they said she had stabbed her husband in the back. She had broken umbrellas, and if she saw a group of children she would shriek and roar and run at us, and we would tear off, terrified. She came up our road a few times, and around Dennehy's Cross. They say she lived in Glasheen, and in my mind she may well be the same woman Paddy saw around Green Street in the 1950s. Maybe not. My own mother, Mary, worked as a psychiatric nurse in Our Lady's Hospital. 'The Mad House', it was called, or 'The Red-Brick'. When my father died so suddenly, and we were all so small, she used to say that her greatest fear was of losing her mind. I was afraid of The Mad House, and never went there. I'm not afraid of going mad any more.

I sing this song and people laugh. The first time I sang it and they laughed, I was shocked. How cruel. Let them laugh, though. It's a funny kind of laugh; there's a lot of recognition in it, and loads of fear, disguised as laughter.

Orca, Orca, Killer Whale

Well, I woke up this morning, and you won't believe
    what I did see,
Three whales outside my window, swimming in the
    River Lee,
Orca, orca, killer whales!

Three whales swam up our river, up through Passage West,
Well, you never saw such excitement,
Nobody had ever seen or heard of such a thing
    before!
People came from far and near to see the whales,
They came on aeroplanes from Finland,
On helicopters from England,
From the radio and the TV.

Well, I met an old woman in the supermarket,
She said, 'John! You have to write a song about the whales!

Who else is going to do it?' I went:
'Orca! Orca! Killer whale!'

Well, I met a busker up on Paul Street,
He said, 'John, I think they come with a message from
  the deep!
Clean up the sea!'
I said, 'I don't know, maybe they just come up for the
  salmon and the mullet,
 I'm not sure!'
But it's true that they spent a long time outside the
  City Hall,
Speaking to the city fathers in a language no one could
  understand.

Three boys come out of Charlie's, one o'clock in the
  morning,
Out of their head on Es,
Well, they thought, ladies and gentlemen, that they took
  one too many,
When they see the three whales splashing around
  outside in the Lee!
Orca, orca, they were killer whales!

Well, the word went out that night on the human-
  mammal mobile phone,
The human mammal gathered from far and near that
  night down on Union Quay,
For the greatest party that was ever held in Cork,
Burning on through the night!
There was drink, there was drugs,

There was music, there was love,
There was whales!
Orca, orca, killer whales!

Well, they swam up as far as the School of Music,
Everybody was getting fierce worried about the whales,
The crowd from the university came on the radio,
They said, 'We have to turn the situation around.
We have to save the whales!'
But they came all the way up to the School of Music,
They came a long, long way, especially to hear
The human children playing the violin!
Orca, orca, they were killer whales!

Well, you never saw such excitement,
The town was full of stories, the city was full of talk,
Old fellahs were going around saying,
'When I was a young fellah you could walk across the
    River Lee
On the backs of the mullet!'
Now the Irish we don't eat the mullet,
We think that they eat the shit off the bottom!
I betcha they're grand, I betcha there's nothing wrong
    with those fish,
The French, for example, love them! So does the
Orca, orca, killer whale!

Well, they hung around for about a week and a half,
Lashing into the salmon and the mullet,
Coming and going as they pleased,
Splashing around in the River Lee,

Underneath the bridges of Cork,
Like they owned the place!

Then the word came through on the radio,
That there was another thirty orca killer whales,
Down by the mouth of the harbour,
What's going on?
There was a pod of whales down in the harbour,
That was the word, that week in Cork you had to have
    the word,
Everyone was going around saying 'pod'.

Then the word came through on the radio,
That Mama Orca died.
She was washed up by Poll Gorm,
Well, the sky was completely blue,
The sea was completely blue,
The day that Mama Orca passed away.
There was a girl crying on the radio.
It's hard for you to imagine, ladies and gentlemen,
And you reading these words, like, in this book,
How upset the people got that time in Cork,
These three whales, they were after swimming into the
    people's hearts!
There was a girl crying on the radio!

Well, the crowd from the university came back on,
They said it was a tooth infection killed the old
    grandmother whale in the end,
Poisoned the blood,
There's no dentist down under the sea, they said,

If you live a long and healthy life, they said,
Death is gonna get you in the end,
Death comes in through the teeth!

Well, the other two whales, they turned around,
They were after learning all her songs.
They swam away back down the harbour,
They met the other thirty orcas waiting for them below,
By the mouth of the harbour,
'Sorry about your mother!'
Then they all turned around and they swam away back
    out to sea,
And they were never seen again!
What was that all about, like?

Well, ladies and gentlemen, that was the summer of the
    whales,
It was only the summer before, the summer before,
The summer before, the summer before,
Last summer!
But now it's just a vague memory with us,
The strange people of Cork,
We've the memory of a goldfish!
But I met an old woman in the supermarket,
She said, 'John, you have to write a song about the
    whales!'
Only for her, ladies and gentlemen, there would be no
    song,
If you could call it a song, like, anyway, I just went:
Orca! Orca! Killer whale!

The first song I got asked for was 'Orca, Orca, Killer Whale'. My song about the cherry blossoms was on the radio a lot that year and everyone was talking about it. I went into the supermarket in Passage West one morning and this old woman started talking to me about the whales that were in the river at that time. 'You have to write a song about the whales, John,' she said, 'Who else is going to do it?'

She looked me in the eye.

'I will,' I said.

She kind of caught me unawares, like, but I had said yes, and now what was I going to do? Write it or not write it? I went through the following thought process: 'No, I couldn't possibly write a song about whales. Why not give it a go? No. Yes. I couldn't. You could.' I gave it a go, and I wrote the song. Yes wins. I remember when I was small at home, there was a book in the house called *The Power of Positive Thinking*. I never actually read it, like, but I got the vibe. Positivity wins.

I have written a lot of 'asked-for' songs now, including 'Passage West', 'The Ballad of Patrick Murphy', 'My Lovely Smiling Beamish Boy' and 'The Streets of Ballyphehane'. It can be a lonely enough ol' road, the songwriting, but the asked-for song takes you outside of yourself and makes you part of a community. It's better to be a giver than a taker. That old woman who asked for the orca song was Rita Forde, and she has passed away since, God rest her soul.

The Moon Going Home

As we were facing down to the river of darkness,
I called on the night to protect us,
As we were together, and as it was us,
A great white moon rose before us.

Ah, just one kind look from the lady of the lamp,
Lean down from the sky to guide us,
A faded flower in her lily-white hand,
On her long, slow dance towards her lover.

It's the moon going home, her face in the clouds,
A great crowd of stars all around her,
She comes to her window, with a candle in her hand,
On her long, slow dance towards her lover.

It's the moon going home,
It's the moon going home,
It's the moon going home!

I was walking home with my little girl, Leslie, when she was about two or three years old, and just learning to talk. We were walking down the Low Road in Cork, and she was holding my hand. The moon was up before us in the sky, big and full and bright. You could see the face of the man in the moon, or the woman in the moon, and because it was a windy night, there were clouds scudding across the face, and it looked like she was travelling along very fast through the clouds and bravely facing into the future.

'Look, Dad,' says Leslie, 'It's the moon going home!'

Out of the mouths of babes often come gems. And so, I have always treasured that phrase and that memory.

I tried to write a song about it at the time, but I just wasn't strong enough or saucy enough with my songwriting at that time of my life. Later, when I found all these positive tricks of the trade (see the songwriting workshop on p. 64) and became much stronger and braver, I went back and tried again, and wrote this song in no time. Very simple and straight, like.

This was on my *Hey Dreamer* album, and there was also a very good and successful version recorded by a fine young singer from Dublin called George Murphy on his album *Dreamed A Dream*.

Hey Dreamer

You forgot who you are, you forgot what you are,
You forgot what you're for, you've forgotten.

You forgot where you're from, you forgot where
    you're goin',
You forgot everything, you've forgotten.

Hey dreamer! Where did you leave your dream?
Where did you leave your dream?
Hey dreamer! Where do you hide your dream?
Where do you hide your dream?

You are a star in the night, you are a wave shining bright,
You are a bird in full flight, you've forgotten.

You are a child on the run, you are a ray of the sun,
You are everyone, you've forgotten.

Hey dreamer! Where did you leave your dream?
Where did you leave your dream?
Hey dreamer! Where do you hide your dream?
Where do you hide your dream?

You are a flame in the wind, you are a leaf in the breeze,
You are a song in the trees, you've forgotten.

You are a star in the night, you are a wave shining bright,
You are a bird in full flight, you've forgotten.

Hey dreamer! Where did you leave your dream?
Where did you leave your dream?
Hey dreamer! Where do you hide your dream?
Where do you hide your dream?

The life of a song! Songs sometimes seem to take on a kind of life of their own. They speak to different people in different ways at different times. I like to try various ways of writing a song and sometimes, just for the hell of it, I make stuff up. That is, I come out with things without really knowing what I am saying, or who is saying what to whom. That is how I wrote this song. My friend John Reynolds produced this song and the album *Hey Dreamer* beautifully in London in 2004 and 2005, and this song shone and became a hit on the radio. In 2016 it was used as the big finishing song in a show called *Exile: Songs and Tales of Irish Australia*, written by that great Irish-Australian songwriter Shane Howard. I got to sing it with a big band of musos and a 150-piece choir to a full house of people in Brisbane. There are echoes here of the ancient Irish incantation 'The Song of Amergin' and the ancient Sanskrit 'You are that.'

Cork

'A charming old town with the spire of Shandon, two sides of it limestone and two sandstone, rising above the river ... I can admire as if I were a stranger the up and down of it on the hills as though it had been built in a Cork accent.' – FRANK O'CONNOR

Cork was a great place to grow up. It is a magical city, full of beauty and wonder. I was raised at its very edge, where the city dissolves into the country. At the bottom of our garden in Laburnum Lawn was what we called 'the ditch'. This was a twisted wonderland of hawthorn, elm, wild pear and alexanders. My mother used to send me 'down the ditch' to gather 'kippins' to start the fire. If you could make your way through the ditch, you came to a low wall, which led to a beautiful apple orchard, and beyond the orchard, a meadow, and beyond the meadow, the limestone quarry, and beyond the quarry, the countryside. The quarry became a lake in winter, an underwater world. It's a wonder we were not drowned as we sailed across it on our rafts.

My four brothers and I went to school in St Joseph's on the Mardyke, another wonderful location, where the Lee flowed all along behind the school. We spent many happy school days playing glassy alleys (Cork slang for marbles) in the yard, and fishing footballs out of the river with sticks and stones. There was often a flock of swans at that slow bend in the south channel of the Lee. Once or twice a week, I would make my way to the City Library on Grand Parade, down Mardyke Parade, across Mardyke Street, down Washington Street and into Hanover Street. There was a paper factory there, and it was like looking into a scene from a Dickens novel. Then down along Nicholas Church Lane, the scary part of the journey, peering between the bricks into the dark crypt of Christ Church, past the old graveyard with its shattered tombs and wild cats. Cork city was an exciting and interesting adventure playground, and it was always fascinating to wander down the Coal Quay, through the English Market, or cycle home along the Mardyke, through Fitzgerald's Park. It seems to me now that the high houses and rainy streets of Cork were filled with a cast of dark and mysterious characters.

Here are some of my heroes who have gone over to the other Cork, an imagined other world, the Cork you see reflected in the River Lee: Patrick Galvin, Frank O'Connor, Rory Gallagher, Seán Ó Faoláin, Seán Ó Riada. Here are a few of my favourite Cork writers, alive in the real world; Ger Wolfe, Cónal Creedon, Mick Flannery, Peadar Ó Riada, Jimmy MacCarthy. Rock on, lads, here in this world.

Cork has never lost any of her magic for me, and it was no wonder when I began to write songs that the first good song to fall into my lap was called 'Prince's Street'.

I'm Moving On

I'm moving on, time to be gone,
Good luck and goodbye, I have to fly,
Make lots of money, keep talking funny,
Run in the sun, what's done is done,
This is the end, my fair weather friend,
Goodbye, so long, farewell, be gone!

I'll see you when I do, even if I don't,
I won't think about you, I wouldn't doubt you,
I'll get on without you, don't think I won't,
I have to go, you have to know,
My fine feathered friend, this is the end,
Goodbye, so long, farewell, be gone!

Keep being you, do what you do,
Take what you want, want what you take.
Goodbye and farewell, time is going to tell,

Hope it all works out, what's it all about,
Who said to who? I said to you!
Goodbye, so long, farewell, be gone, I'm moving on!

Go and be happy, better make it snappy,
You have no fear, I won't be here,
I'm going to be gone, if you hear a song,
Laughing in the breeze, smiling in the trees,
It might be me, I might be free,
Goodbye, so long, farewell, be gone, I'm moving on!

This is the first song on the 2005 album *Hey Dreamer*. It was the beginning of a new era. I travelled to London and began working with producer John Reynolds in Notting Hill. I've always loved the work of Damien Dempsey, and was delighted to hear the great job John Reynolds made of his music. I rang John up; he had just recorded a new version of my song 'All the Ways You Wander' with Pauline Scanlon. 'Come on over,' he said. John is a great-hearted producer and drummer, and a wonderfully positive man. I have made three albums with him so far and look forward to working with him again. John brought in an inspiring group of musos to play on this album, like Clare Kenny on bass, Caroline Dale on cello and Justin Adams on electric guitar. We walked in Hyde Park every morning, recorded all day and went for a pint in The Cow at night. It was a good time and a big boost for me to work with John and his gang.

The Wild Flowers

'Twas the wild flowers I preferred, who owed nothing to
    nobody,
Who blossomed in the ditches, and made their own way
    in the world.
'Twas the wild flowers I admired, who never done
    nothing to you,
But driven from the garden, they sang their own songs
    in the spring.

You can have your lily, you can have your rose,
That were taken and broken,
And bred by men, they were grafted and lamed,
Twisted and tamed.

But the wild flowers I admired, they had nothing to do
    with you,

They flowered by the roadside, and they wore their own
   colours in the sun.

That were there before you, will be there after you,
That will out, that will out.
Like your own true nature, you can try, you can try,
That you never will defeat.

The wild flowers I admired, they had nothing to do
   with you,
But banished from the garden, they made their own
   way in the world,
They wore their own colours in the sun,
And they sang their own songs in the spring.

Well, you know me, ladies and gentlemen – well, you don't, but
pretend anyway, like – I'd write a song about anything, and here's
a song that I wrote about the weeds growing along the side of
the road. Some people say this is my song. 'That's the song that'll
live after you, John!'

There Was a Man Who Took a Wife

There was a man who took a wife,
To walk beside him through his life,
They walked through sunshine and through rain,
They walked through pleasure and through pain.

She wore a dress of yellow gold,
She was a wonder to behold,
And underneath a purple sky,
She was the apple of his eye.

And when the moon arose in flight,
And stars went blazing in the night,
They crept into each other's dream,
And slept beside a silver stream.

They flew together through the air,
And landed on a distant shore,

They walked along a golden strand
They walked together hand in hand.

She was not the easiest woman in the world,
To get along with, if you understand,
But then again, on the other hand,
He may not have been the easiest man.

But when the moon arose in fright,
And stars went blazing in the night,
They crept into each other's dream,
And slept beside a silver stream.

The world will turn and the rivers flow,
The sun will shine and the winds will blow,
While angels in the afterglow,
Will light their candles in the snow.

There was a man who took a wife,
To walk beside him through his life,
They walked through sunshine and through rain,
They walked through pleasure and through pain.

She wore a dress of yellow gold,
She was a wonder to behold,
And underneath a purple sky,
She was the apple of his eye.

This is one of the few songs for which I wrote the music before the words. From just messing around on the guitar, I found this piece that was very attractive to play. There's something lovely about the chord of E minor; certain notes dance off each other in lovely ways. And so I had the tune of the song for quite a while, but I didn't know what words to sing to it.

Anyway, summer came and I went out the Lee Fields for a swim. I went to one of my favourite places, called the Hell Hole, a most beautiful spot, God's own acre as they call it, and I plunged into the River Lee. Well, there I was, up to my neck in the cold, black river water, and next thing these words came tumbling out of my mouth. I swear. I just said them, I don't know where they came from. 'There was a man who took a wife, to walk beside him through his life, they walked through sunshine and through rain, they walked through pleasure and through pain.' It was a 'Wow' moment. I had gotten married alright, like, to my wife. But I wasn't thinking. I was kind of chanting, or intoning. Like an aerial picking up a signal. Any kind of writing that comes like that is special, I think. You don't know where it came from. There is something very right about it. It has to be right, because you didn't do anything, good or bad, to it, only received it.

I love singing this song at my gigs. I love singing the line about the stars going blazing in the night. I could play the guitar music to this song all day and all night and be happy doing that, but I suppose we can't just do that. We have to get up and get out and earn a few bob as well.

I've already sung this one at quite a few weddings. Ah, sure it's a great honour that people would choose this song for their big day out.

Gortatagort

I sing the fields, I sing the farm,
I sing the house, my mother was born
In Gortatagort, Colomane, a green jewel,
Sewn in a patchwork quilt of fields,
Between the mountain and the river,
In this time now and in another,
Where I ran free with my brothers,
Through the long meadow, the *cnocán rua*,
The fort field, the *páirc na claise*,
The new house field, the *gallán* field,
The clover field, the rushy field.

Where the red fuchsia weeps in the hen's garden,
And the angels bleed over Bantry Bay.

I see the house, I see the yard,
I see the stall, I see the stable,

I see the haggard and the hen's garden,
I see the hill, I see the well,
I sing the spring and the well water,
The flat field, the hilly field,
The south ray grass, the north ray grass,
The brake and the *páircín na heornan*.

Where the red fuchsia weeps in the hen's garden,
Where God goes to sleep in the hills and valleys,
And the moon rises over the haggard,
And peace descends on Gortatagort,
And the angels bleed over Bantry Bay.

Ah, saddle up the old grey mare!
Tim Big Danny and Jackie Timmy,
Are going to ride across the mountains to Puck Fair.

I sing the fields, I sing the farm,
I sing the house, my mother was born
In Gortatagort, Colomane, a green jewel.

Gortatagort comes from the Irish *Gort an tSagairt*, 'field of the priest', and is the name of the farm my mother comes from near Bantry, County Cork. I wrote this song after my uncle Tim, my hero, the farmer, died in 2005. It is an elegy for him and for my mother and for the great times we had on the farm as kids. I released it on an album called *My Dark Rosaleen and the Island of Dreams* in 2008. I dedicated the album to my mother, Mary, and she died later that same year. That was a very sad old time.

A lovely thing that happened then was Christy Moore falling in love with this song, and learning and singing it. I invited him down to the farm and we had such a lovely day there visiting my aunt Mary in the old farmhouse. There in the kitchen, Mary played some tunes on the fiddle, I sang 'Gortatagort' and Christy sang 'The Cliffs of Dooneen'. The big old clock was ticking away on the wall. My aunt Chrissie was there. It was like a dream, and it seemed to me that I had been on the right track all my life, following the music along, and had come to this place where I brought Christy Moore to Gortatagort, my mother's home place. I have loved Christy's singing since I was a small boy listening to all those amazing Planxty albums. In later years, he has visited my life with a huge amount of positive energy, and he sings a most tender and beautiful version of this song.

I have great memories of childhood days on the farm with my brothers. I remember rattling away down the boreen on the horse and cart at the end of a long summer's day spent saving the hay, with my uncle Tim and my brothers Maurice and Gerard. I loved the horse and cart.

I remember the start of the summer and Tim going out to catch the horse. I remember Dolly the mare was enjoying the spring grass in the flat field, and did not want to be caught and harnessed for the summer's work.

I remember the big open turf fire and the big black iron kettle hanging over it from the crane, and our grandma sitting beside it. She was born in the nineteenth century.

I remember my uncle Tim, the diviner, breaking a rod from the sally trees in the hen's garden and it jumping in his hands from the electricity of two streams of water meeting together far down under the ground.

I remember our grandma was old and in Skibbereen

Hospital. We were doing the evening milking and I was sent down to the house to get something or other, and there was a small bird flying around the kitchen. As I tried to shoo the birdeen out of the house, it broke a cup on the dresser. I thought I was going to get blamed for breaking the cup. I went back up to the others and told them about the bird in the house.

'Jesus, Mary and Joseph,' said Aunty Mary, 'She's gone!'

About a half an hour later, a car came up the boreen with the news: our grandma, Christina Minihane from Whiddy Island, had died. That was a sign of death in the country long ago, a bird coming into the house. I was honoured to be visited by that otherwordly experience.

I remember the day a swarm of bees came into the yard. Our uncle, Tim Big Danny, got all us children to get sticks and bang them on buckets, tops of churns and anything metallic. That ringing, metal-banging music would cause the swarm to settle, and when the bees heard it they landed on a tree beside the hennery. Tim got those bees and their queen into a sack. He built them a hive out of a tea chest, and they were there for years after that. He would send us up with a saucer of sugar for them on freezing cold spring mornings. Eventually, I suppose, they rose up and swarmed again, and followed their queen away through the air to some other place that wasn't Gortatagort.

I remember the night the first man landed on the moon, and because we had no telly we travelled over to Dan Cruaidh's house to watch the fuzzy pictures on the big old telly. Then we stepped out into the farmyard and looked up at the moon, knowing there was a man up on it. I was eight years old, that time: a good age.

Rise Up, Lovely Molly

Rise up, lovely Molly, the frost is all over,
Banish misfortune, and away we go.

Some say that I'm foolish, and more say I'm wise,
There is a small enchanted glen that I know,
Apples in winter, banish misfortune,
Oh love, 'tis a cold frozen night and I am covered in
snow.
As I strayed out on a foggy morning, in harvest,
The morning star, the mountain road,
Over high, high hills and lofty mountains,
On a long, long summer's day,
Along with my love I'll go.

If all the young maidens were blackbirds and thrushes,
All the young men would be beating the bushes,

Numbers I've courted and kissed in my time,
I will visit my love on the mountain.
Last night I dreamt of my own true love, the blackberry
blossom.
Rise up, lovely Molly,
Over high, high hills and lofty mountains,
On a long, long summer's day,
Along with my love I'll go.

Rise up, lovely Molly, the frost is all over,
Banish misfortune, and away we go.

This song is made up out of the names of Irish traditional tunes and songs. I have always loved the names of the tunes: 'Over the Moor to Maggie', 'Banish Misfortune', 'Boil the Breakfast Early' – there are thousands of them. I got all the titles in this song from the index of a book called *Petrie's Complete Irish Music*. There are 1,584 melodies in that book and the name of every single one of them is brilliant.

I love Irish traditional music; I mean I really love it. I didn't grow up with it, but I have had a couple of really moving experiences with this music, which I'm going to share with you now, gentle reader.

One night around Christmas, I was in Café Lorca in Cork, and Jackie Daly played a slow air on the melodeon that made the hair stand up on the back of my neck. It was so deep, ancient, sorrowful, Gaelic – like a deep river of emotion. I don't know what air it was, because I didn't know the names of them then, but I think now it might have been '*Seán Ó Duibhir an Ghleanna*'.

In 1981, I was playing a gig one night in Le Havre, France, with Mick Hanly and Máirtín O'Connor. It was a highly charged night. The people of Le Havre had blockaded the port against all British vessels, in protest at the British government's treatment of the hunger strikers and their demands. Máirtín played a slow air called '*A Stór Mo Chroí*' and it was so beautiful, it touched me very deeply. The Irish slow airs are magnificent, soaring, keening cathedrals of light and air. I love Irish traditional music.

The Dunnes Stores Girl

(Words: John Spillane and Louis de Paor,
Music: John Spillane)

Hey, check out the Dunnes Stores Girl,
She's the one who rules my world,
I'm gonna walk down the aisle with the Dunnes Stores Girl,
She rules my world.

I'm gonna walk down the aisle with the Dunnes Stores Girl,
In your dreams, says her brother, he's a skinhead,
And he wants me dead, 'In my dreams is right,' I said,
I'm gonna run down the aisle with the Dunnes Stores Girl,
She rules my world.

Na na na na na na, na na na na na na,
The Dunnes Stores Girl!

She knows we're looking at her, and she knows she's
    looking fine,
And she doesn't have all day, and you have to wait
    in line,
I would wait in line till kingdom come,
For salvation in her smile.

And I'd love to stop that clock, looking down on her all
    the time,
Like a jumped-up little manager in a suit that doesn't
    rhyme,
And you never patronise her, only always idolise her, the
Dunnes Stores Girl.

Na na na na na na, na na na na na na,
The Dunnes Stores Girl!

On a cold and rainy Friday night,
Waiting for the world to close,
When she comes up behind me, so brave and so warm,
I know it'll never rain again, I know it'll never rain again,
On the rebel streets of our dreams.

And she doesn't believe a word that I say,
She laughs when I tell her she's a Saturday in May,
And you never underestimate, you never underestimate,
The Dunnes Stores Girl!

So I went into Dunnes Stores in Douglas Court to buy a plug
for the sink, and this girl working there comes up to me and says,

'You're John Spillane – I love your stuff!' Later, she wrote in the guestbook on my website and signed herself 'The Dunnes Stores Girl'. Her brother also wrote in and signed himself 'The Baldy Man'. I replied 'Ye've great names, lads, ye sound like characters out of a song.' She replied, 'If you're such a brilliant songwriter, John Spillane, why don't you write a song about us so?' I replied, 'I will.' That's how the song came about. It was written as a dare, like. Thanks very much, Clare Cogan, the Dunnes Stores Girl, and Mark Cogan, the Baldy Man!

PART FOUR

The River to the Stars Confessed

Passage West

I met my love in Passage West,
The sun was sinking down to rest,
The river to the stars confessed,
'Twas the dark haired woman I loved best.

We wandered down by the Chapel Square,
And there was magic in the air,
And Mother Nature gently pressed
The burning river to her breast.

I offered her a golden ring,
My hand, my heart and everything,
I offered her a sweet love nest,
By the flowing banks of Passage West.

Oh love, will you go, will you go, will you go?
Or love, will you stay, will you stay, will you stay?

We watched the ferry come and go,
We watched the river ebb and flow,
The tide breathe in, the tide breathe out,
We watched the Passage flowers grow.

The ghostly forms of the hungry years,
In sad procession did appear,
With hope and sorrow made their way,
For their passage west to Americay.

Oh love, will you go, will you go, will you go?
Or love, will you stay, will you stay, will you stay?

The famine queen stood tall and proud,
On either bank the people bowed,
From Passage West came a Fenian yell,
'Rule Brittania, rule in hell.'

The grass grows green on the other side,
And mighty ships sail out the tide,
To far-flung harbours across the sea,
Far away from Passage, my love and me.

Oh love, will you go, will you go, will you go?
Or love, will you stay, will you stay, will you stay?

I met my love in Passage West,
The sun was sinking down to rest,
The river to the stars confessed,
'Twas the dark haired woman I loved best.

I have been living in Passage West, County Cork, for nearly twenty years now, and I remember well the day my neighbour Walty Murphy came towards me on the street, with a book in his hand and a serious look on his face.

'John,' he said, 'Would you ever write a song for Passage West?'

He had an ambassadorial air about him, like. Well, I was delighted with him and I replied, 'Congratulations, Walty, you've certainly come to the right place today, like – welcome to the Hit Factory!'

I spent a long time working on this song. I wrote the verses in Ireland and the chorus in America. It has been covered beautifully by Muireann Nic Amhlaoibh and Danú, by Emily McShane and Girsa, by Caroline Fraher and by others. Thank you, Walty, my Passage muse!

The Ballad of Patrick Murphy

They lived beside the river,
At the turning of the tide,
They lived beside the river,
By the river they lived and they died.

Patrick Murphy was a fisherman,
And a gentleman, was a good man,
In the town of Passage West,
With a wife and seven children,
And he tended to his nets.

In nineteen and eleven,
One lovely night in May,
He rowed with three companions,
Across to French's Bay.

A fishing for a living,
Like their fathers done before,
They were dreaming of the salmon,
As they waited on the shore.

They lived beside the river,
At the turning of the tide,
They lived beside the river,
By the river they lived and they died.

Till the bailiff's boat came down the Lee,
The dreaded Murricawn,
They came down from Blackrock Castle,
They snuck down past the Moocawn.

For the Murricawn were gangsters,
In the service of the Crown,
And they came down with revolvers,
And they shot Pat Murphy down.

Bring in that man who shot me,
Before you and I must part,
I bear no grudge against him,
I forgive him from my heart.

They lived beside the river,
At the turning of the tide,
They lived beside the river,
By the river they laughed and they cried,
By the river they lived and they died.

Two thousand and eleven,
We are gathered on the green,
To remember Patrick Murphy,
In beautiful Toureen.

For the people still remember,
That justice was not done,
For the killing of Pat Murphy,
By a bullet from a bailiff's gun,
By a bullet from a bailiff's gun.

They lived beside the river,
At the turning of the tide,
They lived beside the river,
By the river they laughed and they cried,
By the river they dreamed and they sighed,
By the river they lived and they died.

Well, I wrote 'Passage West' at the request of my neighbour Walty Murphy and it went down great. Then Walty asked me to write another song for him, about his grandfather Patrick who was shot dead by water bailiffs (the Murricawn) in 1911. It was a big story in the headlines at the time. There was a court case and the bailiffs got off scot-free. There was a regatta held in Passage in 1911 to gather money for the Widow Murphy Fund. In 2011, we reproduced that festival and renamed the town park in his honour: Patrick Murphy Park. We had the Barrack Street Band playing and there was a blessing of the boats. Patrick Murphy's many descendants dressed up in period costume, and I performed this newly composed ballad for the occasion.

As I was walking past the dockyard a few days later, this man was walking out of it and he looked at me and asked, 'Are you the bard of Passage West?'

And I said, 'I am.'

This was a favourite song of the late great Páidí Ó Sé from Ventry in County Kerry. I played many great nights of music in Páidí's bar in *Ard a' Bhóthair* the last few years he was there. I'd be driving west, through *Lios Póil* and coming around the hairpin bend at *Log na gCapall*, and there would be the first poster stuck in the ditch – 'John Spillane in Páidí Ó Sé's tonight, 9pm. *Fáilte!*' The next poster would be at *Garraí na dTor*, and so on.

'Will you sing "The Ballad of Patrick Murphy", John?' he'd say.

'I will,' I'd say. 'Who's going to stop me?'

This musical life is full and rich. The craic beats all, like – tearing around west Kerry with Páidí Ó Sé in the 'Silver Bullet', flashing past the reeds in the darkness and the moon up high in the sky, and Páidí going around taking down the posters for the gig. 'The most important thing about putting up the posters, John, is taking down the posters!' I had great craic travelling over the Conor Pass with Páidí, and got great enjoyment out of him. He was hugely positive, encouraging and supportive to me. May he rest in peace.

Another great hero of mine, Christy Moore, performs a tender and beautiful version of this song. The melody is similar to 'The Galtee Mountain Boy', which I would have heard from Christy. It is a fascinating part of the Irish song tradition how it has now gone around in a circle and returned to him in a new form.

The Ferry Arms

Well you'd wanna hear the talk
Outta the mocky shams in The Ferry Arms on a
    Saturday night,
It's a Glasgow Celtic pub alright, the walls are painted
    green and white,
'Thirsty work!' says Christy Burke, 'Pullin' pints of porter!'
'How's the form, mock?'
'Not too bad, mock.'
'What are you having, mock?'

'A Beamish for the mock, and a Baileys for the mock,
Ballygowan for the mock, and a brandy for the mock,
Murphy's for the mock and a Guinness for the mock,
And whatever you're having yourself, mock!'

Irish might be there, The Crab might be there,
Hammer might be there, Bones might be there,

You might be there yourself!
You might meet Noble Shepherd or The Ratcatcher,
Who's that on the wacka tobacca doin' the haka in the
    middle of the floor?
Only Robbie Parata, the Maori man!
Who's that comin' through the door?
Kenny, Daithí, Paki, Jock!
'How's the form, mock?'
'Not too bad, mock.'
'What are you having, mock?'

'A Beamish for the mock, and a Baileys for the mock,
Ballygowan for the mock, and a brandy for the mock,
Murphy's for the mock and a Guinness for the mock,
And whatever you're having yourself, mock!'

Well, the writing is on the wall, from the Treaty of
    Arbroath 1320,
A grave and solemn oath,
'So long as one hundred of us remain alive,
We shall not to any degree be subject to the dominion
    of the English,
For it is not for glory nor riches, nor for honour that we
    fight,
But for freedom, which no man loses,
But with his life!'
'How's the form mock?'
'Not too bad, mock.'
'What are you having, mock?'

'A Beamish for the mock, and a Baileys for the mock,
Ballygowan for the mock, and a brandy for the mock,
Murphy's for the mock and a Guinness for the mock,
And whatever you're having yourself, mock!'

Well you know who you are in The Ferry Arms,
You cannot pretend to be who you are not, in The
    Ferry Arms.
'How's the form, mock?'
'Not too bad, mock.'
'What are you having, mock?'

'A Beamish for the mock, and a Baileys for the mock,
Ballygowan for the mock, and a brandy for the mock,
Murphy's for the mock and a Guinness for the mock,
And whatever you're having yourself, mock!'

I was exploring the idea of writing some songs based on the ups and downs of the Cork accent when I overheard someone calling a round of drinks in my local pub, The Ferry Arms. It is a great pub and Christy Burke is a great barman. The craic and the slagging there are mad, and unbelievable at times. The call sounded like a song, and I just lifted it and made it into this song. We had great fun recording all the locals singing on the chorus, and even more fun making the video for this song. A lot of the characters in the song feature in the video, like The Ratcatcher and The Crab. Passage is great for nicknames. Noble Shepherd is not a nickname, however, but a real name. Thanks, Noble. Thanks to Christy Burke, Rob Parata, The Crab, Bones, Irish, Hammer, Kenny, Paki, Daithí, Jock, Cónal Creedon, Barry

Donnellan, Tony McCarthy, Colin Morrison, Jean Crowley and all the Forefront TV crew. The word 'mock' comes from the Irish *mac*, same pronounciation, which means 'son'. Sometimes you'd hear 'mock', or 'mocko', or 'mocky sham'. Small bits of Irish like that remain in Cork slang.

The Voyage of the *Sirius*

The *Sirius* was a noble ship, she sailed the ocean wide,
She steamed from Passage to New York, and then she
    steamed on home to Cork,
She was the first to make that trip, the *Sirius* was a
    famous ship,
She sailed the ocean wide.

Oh, the wise man said you would as soon send a sailor
    to the moon,
As cross the wild Atlantic by steam, boys, by steam,
But Captain Roberts, he was brave, he liberated many
    slaves,
Chased them slavers round the sea, he was brave, he
    had to be,
He steamed on home to Passage West, set out on his
    golden quest,

The wise man said you would as soon send a sailor to the moon.

But all the bells were ringing, all the people singing,
She steamed up the Hudson River to the heart of old
*   New York,*
To Staten and Manhattan, she tied up in Battery Park,
Hurray, boys, hurray, for the Sirius, *boys, hurray!*

Her figurehead, a small white dog that held a shining star,
The brightest star in all the skies, the day star, the dog
   star, that lovely morning star,
As she sailed off from the wharf, the *Sirius* she was but
   a dwarf,
Compared to the *Great Western*, or to the *British*
   Queen,
But this little paddle steamer brave, she breasted every
   angry wave,
She was the first to make it through, she linked the old
   world to the new.

But all the bells were ringing, all the people singing,
She steamed up the Hudson River to the heart of old
*   New York,*
To Staten and Manhattan, she tied up in Battery Park,
Hurray, boys, hurray, for the Sirius, *boys, hurray!*

'If I could live a thousand years, I'd trade them for this
   day,

I am the toast of all New York,' did Captain Roberts say,
But his story won't be read till the sea gives up her dead,
For an empty tomb in Marmullane pays tribute to this
    gallant man.

But all the bells were ringing, all the people singing,
She steamed up the Hudson River to the heart of old
    New York,
To Staten and Manhattan, she tied up in Battery Park,
Hurray, boys, hurray, for the Sirius, *boys, hurray!*

The *Sirius* was a noble ship, she sailed the ocean wide,
She steamed from Passage to New York, and then she
    steamed on home to Cork,
She was the first to make that trip, the *Sirius* was a
    famous ship,
She sailed the ocean wide.

Passage West, where I live, continues to be a source of inspiration for my songwriting. Having written the song 'Passage West' and the follow-up 'The Ballad of Patrick Murphy', I went on to write 'The Ferry Arms' about a pub in the town, and then in 2013 I was commissioned by the Passage West Maritime Festival to write a song about the *Sirius*, the first steamship to cross the Atlantic from west to east. It's my first maritime number. I am delighted that this song has made it into the repertoire of the sea-shanty group The Mollgoggers from Cobh. They have chanted it at a number of international sea shanty festivals.

Captain Roberts was a Passage West man, a local hero, and he went on to be given the freedom of New York City. It is a fantastic story, which was made into a Hollywood film called *Rulers of the Sea*. You can see the iron shaft of the *Sirius* and read the story of that historic voyage in a little park in Glenbrook near Passage West.

Lover's Leap

About a mile from Mallow town,
There is a place called Lovers' Leap,
A beauty spot of great renown,
A jagged rock that rises steep,
A lonely cliff above the deep
Blackwater.

The gentry planted all these trees,
The oak, the beech and the lonely pine,
And courting couples sometimes please,
To wander there and take their time,
And breathe the beauty,
By the shining river.

About a hundred years ago,
Or so the local people tell,

Under a weight of great sorrow,
A handsome courting couple fell
To their doom inside the dark Blackwater.

Lovers' Leap,
Together in endless peace,
Forever in blissful sleep.

A Catholic and Protestant
Had fallen for each other's charms,
Their families would not consent,
They fled and sought each other's arms,
They sought each other's arms and fled,
And dived into their marriage bed,
Inside the cold Blackwater.

They reached the rocky height that night,
One last kiss, one last embrace,
They cried and held each other tight,
Then stepping into endless space,
They wandered out into the air,
And left this earth for evermore,
And reached the sad Blackwater.

Their bodies wrapped in endless night,
Their souls sailed on into the bright
Encircling stars and the caring moon,
The sun shone down upon their love,
From heaven's branches high above the dark
    Blackwater.

Lovers' Leap,
Together in endless peace,
Forever in blissful sleep.

The priest he offered up the host,
The river offered up the moon,
And Jesus wept to see his name,
Divided in a crazy game,
And Mary sent an angel down,
Who wandered on through Mallow town,
And reached the great Blackwater.

Lovers' Leap,
Together in endless peace,
Forever in blissful sleep.

Sometimes I used to play gigs in a place called the Lodge Bar, just outside the town of Mallow in north Cork. One time I went for a walk around before the gig, and I came across this most beautiful and spectacular spot on the River Blackwater, which flows along behind the pub. It was a huge limestone cliff above the river, all covered in trees, with a small cave at the bottom of it, and the lovely Blackwater flowing quietly by. There was gravel beach, some stunted thorn trees and horses grazing in the fields nearby. A stunning spot.

The next time that I played the Lodge, I says to one of the lads, 'Only that 'tis dark now, Robbie, I would have gone for a walk down to that lovely place on the river.'

Well, Robbie looked at me and says – 'Lovers' Leap!'

'What?' says I.

'Lovers' Leap,' says Robbie O'Callaghan. 'One hundred years ago, in the town of Mallow,' says he, 'a boy and a girl fell in love, but they were not allowed to get married, because they were Catholic and Protestant, so they ran away and took themselves down to that lonesome rock and drowned themselves there, and ever since the place has been known locally as Lovers' Leap.'

Well lads, whatever way he told it, it was like he struck me in the heart with an arrow. It was like Romeo and Juliet. You'd have to know Robbie. He has a way of doing that.

'Oh my God,' says I, 'I'm going to write a song about it.'

And I did, and here it is now. Not exactly a laugh a minute of a song, as you may understand, being all about suicide in the River Blackwater in north Cork. Some of the lines of the song are exactly as they were told to me that night by the locals – 'The gentry planted all these trees.'

As part of my research in writing the song, I explored the history behind the story, to see if there was any factual evidence, or if it was myth.

Myth: something that never happened, but always is.

So I got on to the Mallow Field Club, the county library and local historians, and found, as I expected, that there was no historical evidence to the story. Indeed, one hundred years ago they were probably telling the same story, and that it had happened one hundred years before, and so on back through the mists of time.

I love folklore and mythology. I love the local legends that are to be found throughout Ireland, and I am composing an opera about one of them called *The Legend of the Lough – Finscéal an Locha*. It's an opera in two languages, Irish and English, on two stages, the overwater stage and the underwater stage, in two worlds, this world and the other world! In my dream, it will be performed on the floating stage on the Lough of Cork on Bonfire Night, St John's Eve, and all the people of Cork will gather on the banks of this lovely lake for the occasion, and people will travel there from near and far. Dream on, Johnny boy, dream on!

Folklore and Mythology

Consider the following, gentle reader: in Greek mythology, Orpheus was a poet and singer who played the lyre. He could sing the birds down out of the trees. His wife died of a snakebite and she went down into the underworld. Orpheus was such a brilliant player that he persuaded the god and goddess in charge of the underworld to let him go down and bring her back. He went into the world of the dead, he got past the three-headed dog and he returned, but he could not bring his wife back. He came back alone and was later stoned to death by the women of Thrace. Oisín (the fawn) was our Gaelic Orpheus. He travelled to the other world after Niamh of the Golden Hair. Every day there was equal to a hundred years in our world. He came back after three hundred years had passed in the mortal world, but he didn't last long back here either. Jesus went to the land of the dead, and he came back after three days and three nights. It's all the same story. I love it. Orpheus, Oisín, Jesus, Adonis, Osiris. It's death and resurrection. The return of spring.

I was talking to a local Catholic priest recently, and I suggested to him that the resurrection was mythological and metaphorical. 'You must be reading some very quare books,' he said to me.

St Patrick drove out the snakes. St George defeated the dragon. Zeus defeated Typhon. St Finbarr drove the she-serpent Lugh out of the lake in *Guagán Barra*. It's all the same story. Patrick, Georg, Zeus, Finbarr.

As the English poet Robert Graves put it, when Christianity came to Ireland it was exactly the same as what they had here before; God the Father comes down and impregnates the maiden, using the services of an angel, or a flock of birds – feathers everywhere – and she gives birth to the demigod. His mother is mortal and his father is divine: Cúchulainn, Perseus, Jesus, Hercules, Helen. At school long ago they used to talk to us about the Christians versus the pagans. There is no difference, lads, check it out. You saw it here first!

Some of my favourite books of folklore are *Leabhar Sheáin Uí Chonaill* and *Seanchas Ó Chairbre* – local Cork and Kerry books of folklore, rich in magical stories, journeys and returns of the hero to and from the other world. The little bird that keeps cropping up in these tales, *sprideoigín bhroinndearg de mhuintir Shúilleabháin ó Éirinn* (the little red-breasted sparrow of the O'Sullivan family from Ireland), gives some good advice to the hero on his journeys through the underworld.

Irish mythology is among the most wonderful in the world. Mythology is not to be scoffed at or dismissed, nor is it to be taken literally, factually or historically. But it is to be understood.

A Rock To Cling To

Daddy long legs on the ceiling,
Makes you feel that sad ol' feeling,
Father left and went away,
You won't see him till the judgement day.

Everybody needs a rock to cling to,
Everybody needs a rock.

My mother stood upon the shore,
The ocean gave a mighty roar,
And she turned to face the day,
And to keep the wolves at bay.

Everybody needs a rock to cling to,
Everybody needs a rock.

And she prayed to God on high,
That we would all get by,

So we do the best we can,
Every woman, every man.

Everybody needs a rock to cling to,
Everybody needs a rock.

My daughter dancing on the strand,
And she kicking up the sand,
I have loved her for so long,
That I put her in this song.

Everybody needs a rock to cling to,
Everybody needs a rock.

Hear a man sing to the night,
I love my life, I love my wife,
And I do my work with pride,
With my woman by my side.

Everybody needs a rock to cling to,
Everybody needs a rock.

The little boy who never cried
When his father died,
But went a-hide inside a hollow tree,
And he watched the world go by,
Never stopped to wonder why,
And I turned and he was gone,
Left me here to sing this song.

Everybody needs a rock to cling to,
Everybody needs a rock.

Like 'The Moon Going Home', I had the idea for this song for years, six years this time, before I sat down to write it. I was letting it ferment in the back of my mind, hung from an ol' hook in a small rusty old shed in the back of my mind, so that when I actually went to write the song it all came gushing out in one go.

This is how it happened: In 2003, I did a fantastic tour of the Scottish Highlands, the Shetland Islands and the Orkney Islands. This was put together by two great musical Scots, Andy Shearer and James Henry. James was a Shetlander living in Orkney who used to play in a rocking band called Drop the Box. I played for those lads in the Glasgow Rangers Club in Lerwick, in Kirkwall and in Unst, among other wonderful places. Anyway, I was phoning home to my daughter Leslie, and I was finding it hard to get through, but I got through.

'What are you at?' says James.

'Phoning my daughter,' says I. 'Her mother passed away and I am ringing her every day.'

'Everybody needs a rock to cling to, John,' says he to me, 'Everybody needs a rock.'

And whatever way he said it to me, it was like every word was a hammer, hammered home in that way that only the Scots can do, completely and utterly true; nothing was more certain, and I got it, I completely and utterly got it, that everybody needs a rock to cling to. This is what I call the High Talk. The Scots are brilliant at it. Talk that is spoken in a high fashion and has the wisdom of ages, and is said right. The High Talk. Wonderful to hear it! James Henry, the Shetlander living on Orkney, looks me in the eye and lays bare the whole human race, strips us down to the basic stuff: Everybody needs a rock to cling to. Brilliant! It was after my mother died, then, that I wrote the song.

The Dancer

Yes! She is a dancer,
Yes! A lovely dancer,
Yes! A graceful dancer,
And she has the answer.

She dance, scattering the sunlight,
She dance, wildly in the moonlight,
She dance, happy in the lamplight,
She sparkle like a dancer.

Oh, and when she walk, she float,
And when she float, she shine,
And when she shine,
She dances.

She dance, moving in a dream world,
She dance, even in the real world,

She dance, swaying with whole world,
The wide world over.

Nobody has the answer,
Go now and be a dancer!
Dance sadly in the streetlight,
Dance madly in the firelight.

Oh, and when she walk, she float,
And when she float, she shine,
And when she shine,
She dances.

Nobody has the answer,
Go now and be a dancer,
Dance sadly in the streetlight,
Dance madly in the firelight.

Dance, scattering the sunlight,
Dance, wildly in the moonlight,
Dance, happy in the lamplight,
Sparkle! Like a dancer.

I enjoyed messing around with the English language in this one. She dance. She float. It reminds me of when I used to go to St Joseph's on the Mardyke long ago. The teachers used to be giving out to the boys for not speaking proper English. 'Speak the Queen's English, boy,' they'd say. They meant well. A lot of the kids from the Marsh in Cork, maybe from Hoggy Bah, spoke glorious Cork English, as their parents spoke at home, their mother tongue. 'I seen him when he done it' was the example usually used for this dialect. Later I discovered that this was not 'wrong' English, but a dialect of Elizabethan English that still survives in Cork. That's why we still say 'ye' for you plural. Up Cork! *Corcaigh abú!*

When We Sang

And when we sang, we sang like the stars,
We sang like the wind, we sang like the dark,
We sang like old women weeping in cathedrals,
We sang like whiskey in the jar,
When we sang, we sang like the stars.

And when we sang, we sang like the sun,
We sang like the breeze, floating through the trees,
We sang like quiet spaces in fresh green forests,
The long green corridors of summer,
When we sang, we sang like the sun.

And when we sang, in glorious technicolour,
Of our lives, the time that we spent together,
Where you alone, you are the only hero,
In this movie that you call your life,

And then we bow, and the blossoms come tumbling
  around us,
The curtain falls, darkness will all surround us,
We slip away, and say 'Remember me with love.'

And when we sang, we sang like the sea,
We sang like the moon, we sang like the tide,
We sang like distant palaces by moonlight,
Like cities drowned beneath the starlight,
Like prisoners breaking free,
When we sang, we sang like the sea.

We sang for Ireland and for glory and for home,
We sang for Ireland, we drank for Ireland,
We danced for Ireland and we cried for Ireland,
For Ireland and for glory and for home.

And when we sang, we sang like the stars,
We sang like the wind, we sang like the dark,
We sang like old women weeping in cathedrals,
We sang like whiskey in the jar,
When we sang, we sang like the stars.

This song was inspired by a performance I saw once at the Cork Choral Festival, years ago. I was working on a scheme called the Composer in the Classroom Scheme and writing songs with kids in schools. Our singing was really good, and we had brand new songs. (Will we be brilliant or what?) After our performance, the National Chamber Choir of Ireland came up onto the stage. You'd want to have heard them. They were staggering! They sang this astounding piece called *Stabat Mater*, a long, sorrowful, dark wail, like the moon rising over a long sea of troubles, like old women weeping in cathedrals. I once did a fantastic tour with Nomos of ancient, forgotten and neglected heritage towns in a strange and magnificent country called Portugal. We played in a fairy-tale town called Castelo, an ancient walled town perched on top of a sudden hill in the middle of a scorched plain. While sauntering around the town, I went into a dark and ancient cathedral, and there was an old woman in there, kneeling and praying and weeping. It was the saddest thing you ever saw.

My Lovely Smiling Beamish Boy

When you were young you wished to be
Just like your dad, a Beamish boy,
In a happy family,
And your mother's pride and joy.

Don't you remember me at all?
Can't you hear my lonesome call?
You always were my pride and joy,
My lovely smiling Beamish boy!

The scent of malt hangs in the air,
And there is friendship everywhere,
A lonesome star hangs from the sky,
The holy river flows on by.

Don't you remember me at all?
Can't you hear my lonesome call?

You always were my pride and joy,
My lovely smiling Beamish boy!

Don't you remember me at all?
The Beamish brewery standing tall,
But now a cloud hangs over town,
The Beamish brewery has closed down.

I was asked for this song by Mike Hannon for a film he made called *My Beamish Boy*. The malty smell of porter floated over the south side of Cork for many generations from the Beamish brewery. It closed its doors in 2008 after 217 years. Mike gave me a DVD of interviews with the staff and I found it very moving. His film is called *My Beamish Boy* because the apprentices were known as 'boys' until an older man would retire or pass away. A man could be in his forties with a wife and children, and still be a 'boy' in the brewery. A great warmth exuded from the talk of the brewery workers, great stories and yarns, really heart-warming stuff: 'It was the best job in Cork, it was the best job in Europe, it was the best job in the world!'

Beamish closed down around the same time as my mother Mary died, and I think some of the sadness at her passing found its way into this song. The film was premiered at the Cork Film Festival and later shown on RTÉ television. Other music for the film is by Irene Buckley, and the whole film has a lovely feel about it. The phrase 'my beamish boy' has another resonance for me because it features in one of my favourite poems, 'Jabberwocky' by Lewis Carroll, a classic of nonsense poetry. I was honoured to perform the song at the launch of *Beamish & Crawford: The History of an Irish Brewery* by Diarmuid and Donal Ó Drisceoil.

By the way, they are still brewing Beamish stout and it does taste really good, because they took the master brewers and the recipe, and now make it in the Murphy's brewery on the north side. It is my chosen favourite of the stouts of Ireland! *Sláinte*!

The Irish Language

he Irish language is full of poetry, mythology, music and wisdom. If you ever had any doubts about the brilliance of the Irish people, take one look at the language and you will see it is pure poetry, rich and deep, and pure music.

When you get into it, you can see Ireland from an Irish-language point of view, where place names have meanings: Cork is *Corcaigh*, a marsh, and Dublin is *Dubh Linn*, a black pool. I learned Irish at school, and I always liked it. In Bantry, all the place names were in Irish, and full of mystery and romance: *Trá Líobáin, Cnoc na bhFiach, Stuaicín, Gort an tSagairt, Seisceann, Barr Gorm, Páirceanna* – an endless list of Gaelic word-sounds.

They used to talk of 'the language question', but I'm not sure what the question was. Most of the people of Ireland spoke Irish for a few thousand years. They invented it. Then, gradually, the majority of them changed over to English. In the desperate, hard times of the nineteenth century, they used to beat children for speaking Irish. Then, a generation later, they were beating children for not being able to speak Irish. When most of Ireland got independence from an empire that put Irish down, they tried to bring the language back. That didn't work, as the mother tongue was now English for most people. It's the language your mother speaks when you're swimming around in her womb, and when you're born. Many Irish people feel guilt for not being able to speak Irish. They would love to be able to speak it, but they can't. They find the grammar hard. If they try to speak it, they feel they're going to be bad at it, and we don't like to be bad at things because we are so brilliant, like. It's a lot of work to learn a language that isn't your mother tongue. Speaking the mother tongue is just like breathing the air. You don't even have to try. You learned it at a time you probably can't even remember. So, we have this amazing language that most of us can't speak fluently, but we're keeping it going because it's brilliant. Now we send children to gaelscoileanna to let them solve 'the language question'.

The Irish language has been very good to me. When I left the bank and was hanging around the house being a rock and roller, my mother Mary made a proposition to me. 'Go to college,' she said. 'You have loads of time on your hands. You can do your music and go to college at the same time. I'll pay for it.'

So I went to college and I learned Irish. My mother drove me down to the west Kerry Gaeltacht and I learned a lot of Irish there. Uncle Tim said there was no use in the Irish, but my mother always liked it and sometimes threw Irish phrases into her speech. '*Le cúnamh Dé*,' she'd always say. It took a long time to get the hang of it. I remember walking around Cork and thinking, 'Jesus, I've been learning Irish for years and I still can't really speak it.' Eventually, I got it.

I was given the great honour of my very own radio programme on Raidió na Gaeltachta, *Rogha John Spillane*, which went out at 9 p.m. every Sunday night for about seven years, from 2002 to 2009. *Buíochas mór do* Jeaic Ó Muircheartaigh for that honour. I played a wild mixture of records on that show: flamenco, Chinese, Irish, traditional, punk, *sean nós*, opera, rock, African. Since then, I have done a lot of work for TG4. I've made three albums in Irish, and my biggest selling album so far was called *Irish Songs We Learned at School*.

Make no mistake about it, gentle reader, *a chara, a léitheoir shéimh*: Irish is brilliant. *An Ghaeilge abú*!

Martin's Mad About Fish

Delicious the wishes of fishes in dishes,
Jumps out of the ocean and into the pan,
For Martin the hookery cookery man,
The salmon of knowledge below in the college,
The cod on the rod, the jig on the dish,
The fish is mad about Martin,
And Martin's Mad About Fish.

Exactly nineteen seconds long, this little songeen was commissioned by RTÉ TV as a signature theme for a fish cookery programme of the same name starring chef Martin Shanahan. These words made it onto the wall of Martin's restaurant, Fishy Fishy in Kinsale, County Cork. Fair play to me.

River Lee

You'd wanna be mad to go swimming in the river,
But this summer I've been swimming in the river,
In the sacred waters of the River Lee, and I have been
    washed clean,
And I have been set free!

I have dived into the hellhole
Underneath the sycamore tree,
And I have come back to tell the tale,
That I have swam in the sacred waters of the River Lee,
And that I have been washed clean,
And I have been set free,
And I don't need no church made out of stone.

I have dived into the lake in *Guagán Barra*,
And swam with the monster; the she-serpent Lugh,

Who whipped the holy chalice out of the saint's hand
    long 'go;
The luneen! She broke through the rock and she formed
    the River Lee!
I have swam with the monster in *Guagán Barra* lake,
And I have emerged unscathed,
I have come back to tell the tale,
That I have bathed in the sacred, holy waters of the
    River Lee,
And that I have been washed clean,
And I have been set free,
And I don't need no church made of stone.

I have gone out the Lee Fields, beyond the dinosaur,
To the old men who go there every day,
And they says to me, 'Johnny, boy,' they says,
'Come with us! We walks up and we floats down!'
And they does, they does, but I says,
'Lads, I'm not going with ye! Gimme another ten or
    fifteen years!'
But as I breathe, if I live to tell the tale, I hope to go out
    and be,
One of them old men who goes there every day,
They walks up and they floats down! And they does!

Because I have bathed in the sacred, holy waters of the
    River Lee,
And I have been washed clean, and I have been set free,
And I don't need no church made out of stone,
And I don't need no cult of priests from Rome!

I have swam with the ghosts in Inniscarra graveyard,
And I have emerged once again, totally unharmed,
Unscathed, a few grey hairs alright, like,
But I have bathed in the sacred, holy waters of the
River Lee,
And I have been washed clean, and I have been set free!

I would like to mention some of the beautiful rivers that
pour their tribute into the River Lee,
The Owengarbh, the Shournagh, the Martin, the
Dripsey, the *Sulán*, the only male river in Ireland,
That claims a victim every seven years,
'*Is mise an Sulán fada, fireann. Anois an t-am, cá bhfuil
an duine?*'
Because I have bathed in the sacred waters of the
River Lee,
And I have been washed clean, and I have been set free!

I was playing a midsummer gig in that special place *Guagán
Barra* at the source of the Lee. I was hanging out with Ally Ó
Riada and I dived into the lake for a swim, and I came out
singing this song. I performed the world premiere that very night,
eaten alive by midges in the Marquee. Neil Lucey of the Gougane
Barra Hotel gave me lots of great folklore about the she-serpent
Lugh, who broke through the rock and formed the River Lee.
Everything in all these songs is true.

The English Market Christmas Angel Song

Oh, we played a tune on the Shandon Bells, 'The Isle of
  Innisfree',
Then we rambled down through old Cork town, and
  crossed the River Lee.
The Christmas lights were all sparkling as we sauntered
  down the quay,
Into the English Market and into eternity.

'Mo mhúirnín óg, won't you come home to me?
'Tis by the English Market gates I'll be.'

In the English Market I was born, one cold and frosty day,
As they wrapped me up in a cabbage leaf, I could hear
  the angels say,
'Oh, you will know sorrow, small Cork boy, but you'll
  know joy as well,

Only make your choices wisely, between heaven,
   between hell.

Mo mhúirnín óg won't you come home to me?
'Tis by the English Market gates I'll be.'

I hear the angel voices telling me to be strong,
Here in this English Market Christmas Angel Song.

Then my mother gently dipped me in the fountain of
   pure love,
With her tender heart, she missed one part where she
   held me from above,
Oh, and I have wandered fruitlessly through many a
   desert plain,
But before my song is ended I'll be coming home again,

'Mo mhúirnín óg, won't you come home to me?
'Tis by the English Market gates I'll be.'

And if ever I go back to Cork, I'm gonna go there in the
   spring,
When the leaves are green along the mall, and the
   small Cork sparrows sing.
Oh, or I might go there in autumn time when the leaves
   begin to fall,
And the flag of freedom proudly flies above the City Hall.
Or when Christmas lights are sparkling as we saunter
   down the quay,
Into the English Market and into eternity.

'Mo mhúirnín óg, won't you come home to me?
'Tis by the English Market gates I'll be.'

I hear the angel voices telling me to be strong,
Here in this English Market Christmas Angel Song.

Having gotten the reputation of being a songwriter around Cork, it became a running joke there for a while; if I went into a shop to buy a loaf of bread, the person behind the counter would say, 'Sure you might write a song about it, John!' Writing asked-for songs was my thing, and one day I was having a coffee in Cork's English Market when long-time trader Máire Rose said to me, 'Your name came up there, John, at a meeting of the traders, and it was suggested that we might ask you to write a song about the market.' I was delighted, as I've loved the English Market since I was a boy. When we were small, our mother told us that babies came from the English Market, and that seemed about right, what with all the turkeys, chickens, cabbages and fishes that were hanging around there, and the lovely fountain surrounded by three storks.

I launched this song in the English Market at Christmas in 2014, joined by the UCC Choir. The traders made mince pies, mulled wine and spiced beef for us all. It was like a dream, being in the market at night, and we retired to the Mutton Lane Inn and had a laugh. I was delighted. These songs, sometimes it seems like they go unnoticed, and sometimes they seem so big and important – who knows, like? This song seemed to have a resounding effect on certain people who were deeply moved by it. Thank you so much, all the marvellous traders of the deep, dark, magical and mysterious English Market.

A wonderful thing happened when I was writing this song. I composed the verse about the fountain – 'Then my mother gently dipped me in the fountain of pure love, / With her tender heart, she missed one part where she held me from above' – and I was walking in Blackrock when I met Stephen Daunt, a great English teacher. He asked me was I writing anything, so I recited my new verse and told him how I had based it on the myth of Achilles' heel.

'My middle name is Achilles,' he told me, 'It's an old tradition in my family.'

And so I met Achilles in Cork, just as I had composed a verse about him.

PART FIVE

Spillane the Wanderer from Town to Town

Johnny, Don't Go to Ballincollig

Johnny, don't go to Ballincollig,
Where you always get so disappointed,
Johnny, don't go, Johnny, don't go, Johnny, don't go,
Stay in town.

Johnny, don't go to Carrigaline,
Or I'm not coming with you this time,
You only go to get let down,
Johnny, don't go, Johnny, don't go, Johnny, don't go,
Stay in town.

Johnny, don't go calling that woman,
You know she left you behind,
If you go and call that woman,
I'm not coming with you this time,
Johnny, don't go, Johnny, don't go, Johnny, don't go,
Stay in town.

If you go up to Mallow,
Better beware of the big Blackwater,
If you go as far as Mallow,
You might never again come down,
Johnny, don't go, Johnny, don't go, Johnny, don't go,
Stay in town.

Johnny, don't go to the banks of the Shannon,
Johhny, don't go to the banks of the Nile,
Johnny, don't go to London Tower,
Hang around another while,
Johnny, don't go, Johnny, don't go, Johnny, don't go,
Stay in town.

Johnny, don't go to the Crystal Palace,
Johnny, don't go to the hole in the wall,
Johnny, don't go to the big television,
Hey Johnny, don't go at all,
Johnny, don't go, Johnny, don't go, Johnny, don't go,
Stay in town.

WHERE would you be going?
Where WOULD you be going?
Where would YOU be going?
Where would you BE going?
Johnny, don't go, Johnny, don't go, Johnny, don't go,
Stay in town.

Johnny, don't go to Carrigaline,
Or I'm not coming with you this time,

You only go to get let down,
Johnny, don't go, Johnny, don't go, Johnny, don't go,
Stay in town.

Johnny, don't go to Ballincollig,
Where you always get so disappointed,
Johnny, don't go, Johnny, don't go, Johnny, don't go,
Stay in town.

Well, I had heard a lot about this thing called *sean-nós* singing, so I decided to have a go off it. I had good Irish, and I went to a few masters, knelt at their feet and learned how to sing in the *sean-nós* style. I went to Tomás Ó Canainn and Pól Frost, but it was Peadar Ó Riada who really gave me the blessing. He taught me a song called '*Plúirín na mBan Donn Óg*'. 'As for the ornamentation,' he said, 'that will come to you naturally because we are Irish and we have racial memory.' Peadar lives in the Gaeltacht and speaks Irish as his first language. He has been steeped in Irish music and singing all his life, as well as leading the fabulous Cór Chúil Aodha, so when he gave me the go ahead, who was going to stop me? So I put together a certain repertoire of *sean-nós* songs. While I was playing with Nomos, sometimes I would do *sean-nós* versions of rock or jazz songs for fun. This is how I came upon my *sean-nós* version of Chuck Berry's 'Johnny B. Goode', which later metamorphosed into 'Johnny Don't Go to Ballincollig'. Chuck's chorus of 'Go, go, Johnny, go, go!' became 'Johnny, don't go, Johnny, don't go, Johnny, don't go, stay in town.' This is one of the places this song came from.

The more places a song comes from, the stronger the song, I always think. This song also comes from a longing to sing about Irish places and place names. There are so many American songs about places we have never seen: can we not sing about our own, real places? I mean, if you can sing about 'By the time I get to Phoenix', can you not sing about 'By the time I get to Bishopstown'? Is one place any better than another place, really? Every savage loves his native shore.

I've had a long and interesting relationship with the town of Ballincollig, since I was a small boy in Wilton, about three miles away. We were always going there for one reason or another: for fun, on the 'lang' from school, picking fruit at the fruit farms, working for farmers in the summertime, picking potatoes, weeding beet. We had great times cycling out to the castle there and lighting fires. I often enjoyed walking home from Ballincollig when I was young.

Beautiful Ballincollig

Once upon a time, when I was a young fellah,
About eleven or twelve, one place we used to go,
Was called Ballincollig Castle,
It was a most beautiful place.
We'd get together in the morning, round up the
    bicycles,
Myself, Dave Murph, Johnny Isaac, Davy Isaac,
    Brendan Holland,
Maybe Richie Leonard, Jimmy O'Hea, and we'd ride out
    of town,
Bozo the dog running along behind the bicycles,
In case we got attacked, he was a massive dog,
Nobody knew who owned Bozo,
But he'd follow those Isaac boys to the ends of the
    earth,
Anyway, we'd stop at the shop, and we'd ride out of town,

Out into the countryside,
Well, the sun would be shining, the birds would be
     singing,
Out to Ballincollig, up the back road, past the mill,
Down the hill, through the gap, and there,
Three fields across, there she stood;
Beautiful Ballincollig Castle,
All shining in the morning sunlight,
All gentle and noble,
Like an ancient castle from a fairy tale!

Well, we took the castle, we defended the castle,
We fought and died for Ireland in Ballincollig Castle,
We climbed the tower, we lit the fire!

Anyway, next thing, next thing,
The sun climbed up high into the sky,
And rolled down the other side,
And that day ended,
And the following day ended,
And time went by,
And next thing, next thing,
Unbelievably, incredibly!
I grew to be a man!
And I forgot all about that time in Ballincollig Castle.
Until one day, I happened to be out that way,
And I thought I would go and give the old castle a visit,
And see how things stood with her.

Well, I drove in my car out to Ballincollig,
Up the back road, past the mill, down the hill,
No mill now anymore,
Only a big load of apartments called The Granary,
Anyway, down the hill, looking for the castle,
Out the road, back in the road,
No sign of any castle,
I met a man by the side of the road,
'Where's the castle?'
'Ah,' he said, 'It's very hard to get to it now,' he said,
'Over there behind the trees.'
Because, ladies and gentlemen,
A great forest of houses had grown in all the fields
around Ballincollig,
Since I was a boy,
And a great forest of thorn trees had grown,
All around the old castle itself.
Well I fought my way through the thorns,
And, scratched and bleeding,
I stumbled at last on the old keep,
And there she stood,
As beautiful as ever!

Beautiful Ballincollig Castle!
All shining in the morning sunlight,
All gentle and noble,
Like an ancient castle from a fairy tale,
About a million crushed and battered beer cans,
Shining like gold and silver in the morning sunlight,

All around her feet!
Well, I walked around,
And the memories came rushing back,
I was wondering what happened the lads?
I climbed the tower,
And I fell into a dream,
And there,
In the topmost turret,
Of the topmost tower,
Of Ballincollig Castle,
I saw
The most beautiful woman you have ever seen in your
    whole life,
Lying there on a bed of roses,
'John!' she said,
'I thought you'd never get here!'
'I know!' I said,
'Life's been tough. But here I am now!'
Anyway, at that exact second,
A freezing wind, a chilling wind,
A bitter wind, a poison wind,
Blew through the cold, stone,
Glassless windows of the tower,
And I turned around,
And she was gone!

Anyway, where was I? Oh yes!
Anyway, about ten days later,
I happened to be inside in this pub in town,

And I was introduced to this woman,
We were introduced by a poet called
    Diarmuid Ó Dálaigh,
That doesn't matter, anyway,
I recognised her instantly
As the woman I had glimpsed
In my vision in the tower.

After that, ladies and gentlemen,
We got to know each other,
And then, eventually,
We fell in love,
Slowly but surely.
And then, after that, we lived,
For a long time together,
Together, for a long time,
After that, we lived,
Happily ever after!

Bhuel, a dhaoine uaisle, sin é mo scéal,
Is má tá bréag ann bíodh!
Is mise a chum agus a cheap,
Agus ní bhfuair mé dá bharr,
Ach bróga ime agus stocaí páipéir!

Yes, ladies and gentlemen,
That's my story and I'm sticking to it!
If there's any lies in it,
They can stay there now!

All I got for it,
Was a pair of silver wings,
A golden crown,
And a place in heaven!

I got into a lot of trouble for writing 'Johnny, Don't Go to Ballincollig', especially with certain people from the town of Ballincollig, who actually weren't a bit impressed. Well, I made them a solemn promise that I would write a follow-up song called 'Beautiful Ballincollig' and that it would be a far superior song, both in lyrics and in melody. So I often went out to the town of Ballincollig, walked around, looked at the sky, looked at the ground, waiting for inspiration to strike, and it never happened. Eventually, under fierce pressure, under enormous pressure, I managed to write this song called 'Beautiful Ballincollig'. It was 100 per cent perspiration, 0 per cent inspiration that went into this song and it's finally finished now, after five years of hard work inside in the Hit Factory. The words are finally finished now, done and dusted, off by heart, and the melody is absolutely beautiful, even though I say so myself – too good for them actually, if the truth be known!

Life in an Irish Town

Yes, it rains, it rains a lot, you got to be grateful for
what you've got,
Yes, it rains, it rains on down, sometimes I worry, we'll
all be drowned,
But when it shines, and it does shine, but when it shines;

It is the most beautiful island on God's green earth,
The most beautiful island gave you birth,
That's life, life in an Irish town, just life,
Life in an Irish town,
One day you're up and the next you're down,
Life in an Irish town,
Put on your smile, don't wear your frown,
Life in an Irish town.

Yes, it rains, cats and dogs, soft day, thank God,
Yes, it rains, six inch nails, sometimes I worry, we'll be
washed away,
But when it shines, and it does shine, but when it shines;

It is the most beautiful island on God's green earth,
The most beautiful island gave you birth,
That's life, life in an Irish town, just life,
Life in an Irish town,
One day you're up and the next you're down,
Life in an Irish town,
Put on your smile, don't wear your frown,
Life in an Irish town.

You gotta cool down, calm down, climb down, tone down,
Back down, track down, wolf down, wash down,
Slow down, touch down, steady down, knuckle down,
Buckle down, write down, whittle down, settle down,
Life in an Irish town!

It was a great honour for me to present my own series on TG4, our Irish language TV channel, in 2013 and 2014. It was called *Spillane an Fánaí*, which means 'Spillane the Wanderer'. I got the gig off Tony McCarthy and his dad Joe, who have a company called ForeFront Productions. For many years they produced an iconic series for TG4 called *Geantraí*. This was traditional music sessions from pubs all around Ireland. *Geantraí* came to an end, and Tony and Joe approached me with this idea: I would go and visit a number of small towns in Ireland and use one of the really good pubs in the towns as my headquarters. I would work behind the bar and get to know the local characters, learn about the history, music and folklore of the town. They suggested that I might write a few lines of a song about the town then as well. It was my own idea to write a full song about each town. Tony never put me under pressure to do that. I took over my own series from the inside and turned it into one big songwriting workshop. We had a lovely crew on the road, and we met great and colourful characters around the small rural towns of Ireland. I released an album of the songs from the first series called *Life in an Irish Town* in 2013 and an album the following year called *The Man Who Came in from the Dark*. I am very proud of these town songs. Happy days in the Hit Factory, lads, putting the ball in the back of the net, left, right and centre – fair play to me.

Graiguenamanagh

*Graiguenamanagh, Graiguenamanagh, on the banks
    of the shining Barrow,
I found peace in Graiguenamanagh, at the side of that
    lovely stream.*

There were three sisters flowing, gently going, the Suir,
    the Nore, the Barrow,
There were three rivers flowing, down to the salty sea.

*Graiguenamanagh, Graiguenamanagh, on the banks
    of the shining Barrow,
I found peace in Graiguenamanagh, at the side of that
    lovely stream.*

There were three sisters weaving, and receiving, the
    Suir, the Nore, the Barrow,
There were three sisters weaving, down to the salty sea.

Graiguenamanagh, Graiguenamanagh, on the banks
  of the shining Barrow,
I found peace in Graiguenamanagh, at the side of that
  lovely stream.

There were three sisters dancing, and romancing, the
  Suir the Nore, the Barrow,
There were three sisters dancing, down to the salty sea.

Graiguenamanagh, Graiguenamanagh, on the banks
  of the shining Barrow,
I found peace in Graiguenamanagh, at the side of that
  lovely stream.

I was heading for Graiguenamanagh, County Kilkenny, to make
a show for TG4 about that lovely town. I tried singing the word
Graiguenamanagh, up and down, this way and that way, and I
made up a little melody. I had a good start made before I even
got there. I arrived the night before the rest of the crew and so I
had time to work it out. I learned at school long ago about the
three sisters, the Suir, the Nore and the Barrow, and that was a
good way to go with the song. I also called them Yesterday, Today
and Tomorrow, which I was proud of, and which rhymed, and I
had them weaving and receiving, going and flowing 'down to the
salty sea'.

    We had a good ol' time in Graigue'. We were based in Doyle's
Bar, and went sailing up the Barrow in a barge, singing songs.
Next thing, Leo Moran of The Saw Doctors arrived in and we
had a mighty sing-song. It's a great life, this musical life.

Fethard Town

As I went down through Fethard town,
In the County Tipperary,
I met the goose on the loose, and she mutterin' and
    stutterin',
The dander of the gander and he goin' to reprimand her,
What's the use of a truce with the goose on the loose?
Peace with the geese, and they feathered in Fethard.

In Fethard town, in Fethard town,
The sun goes up, the sun goes down,
The auld Clashawley flows around,
I wish I was in Fethard town.

As I went down through Fethard town,
In the County Tipperary,
I met the *Síle na Gig* and she dancing a jig,

She clingin' to the wall and she laughin' at them all,
Sayin' they'll never understand me,
Ah, the mystery of history, the hassle in the castle,
The monk in the bunk, the skill with the quill,
And it feathered in Fethard.

In Fethard town, in Fethard town,
The sun goes up, the sun goes down,
The auld Clashawley flows around,
I wish I was in Fethard town.

As I went down through Fethard town,
In the County Tipperary,
I met a mouse with a horse and he trainin' him of
    course,
For the big gold cup, giddy up, giddy up,
The thoroughbred blood and the Coolmore stud,
The party at MacCarthy's and the fiddle and the
    griddle and the riddle,

What made the hearse horse hoarse?
The COFFIN of course!
And the undertaker under, take her under, undertaker,
And the undertaker under, take her under, undertaker,

And the mouse in the house, the goose on the loose,
The horse in the box and the hassle in the castle,
The *Síle na Gig*, she dancin' a jig,
The monk in the bunk, and it feathered in Fethard.

In Fethard town, in Fethard town,
The sun goes up, the sun goes down,
The auld Clashawley flows around,
I wish I was in Fethard town.

With the fí ard, bí ard, crann ard, coill ard, sliabh ard,
*   riamh ard,*
Nuair a chacann gé, cacann siad go léir,
Ar thaobh na gréine de Shliabh na mBan!

This song is not as nonsensical as it seems. The mouse with the horse, for example, is Mouse Morris, a champion horse trainer. The goose on the loose refers to the town geese in Fethard, a wonderful walled heritage town with actual town geese. They were a bit of a nuisance hanging around the chipper at night, and I'm not sure how many of those geese are now left. The riddle – 'What made the hearse horse hoarse?' – I learned from Colm Murphy, the bodhrán player, in the Corner House bar on Coburg Street in Cork.

Castleisland

In a castle on an island, in a kingdom long ago,
A maiden in her garden was playing in the snow.

A ring upon her finger, was a ring of Spanish gold,
Her crimson cloak wrapped round her, to keep her
    from the cold.

In a castle on an island, on an island in a stream,
A stream within a kingdom, a kingdom in a dream.

A' sprideoigín bhroinndearg de mhuintir Shúilleabháin
Ó Éirinn taobh thiar di, do labhair ar an mbán,

'Ansan ataoi a mhaighdean, ar Oileán Chiarraí,
Is ardaigh suas do mhisneach, is slánaigh do chroí.'

Castleisland, Castleisland,
On an island in a stream,
A stream within a kingdom,
A kingdom in a dream.

'A mhaighdean mhín mhánla,
I gcaisleán an rí,
Mar rós i lár an tsneachta,
Ar Oileán Chiarraí.'

Castleisland, Castleisland,
On an island in a stream,
A stream within a kingdom,
A kingdom in a dream.

In a castle on an island, in a kingdom long ago,
A maiden in her garden, was playing in the snow.

A ring upon her finger, was a ring of Spanish gold,
Her crimson cloak wrapped round her, to keep her from
the cold.

A lovely thing happened around the writing of this Castleisland song. I made up the idea of the castle on the island in the stream in the kingdom, and I put in one of my favourite folklore motifs, the little red-breasted robin of the O'Sullivan people from Ireland, which is a Kerry thing. I wrote this before we went there to film the episode of *Spillane an Fánaí*, to take the pressure off myself, like.

When we reached the castle in Castleisland, we were in a lovely little garden under the castle walls where boys were playing, and this man came out and told us a story out of the blue about his father, who used to work that garden. He always had a little red-breasted robin going along beside him, picking the worms, and he was practically tame. 'Anyway, the old man died and on the first anniversary of his death a robin came into the house and landed on my father's picture.' I hadn't said anything at all about a robin, but I had the robin in the song before I got there, and the robin was there ahead of us in the story.

Kiltimagh – The Dark Wind from the Mountain

Kiltimagh, Kiltimagh, the dark wind from the mountain
Is searching through the streets down town.
Kiltimagh, Kiltimagh, all your lovely sons and daughters
Are scattered now like the thistledown.

Oh, Coillte Mách, a mhíle grá, we'll linger here a while,
By the shadow of that old Sliabh Chairn.
Roses bloom, roses bloom, all along the Yellow River,
One childlike star steps out into the dawn.

All my dreams, all my dreams, I dreamed them in the
    morning,
I dreamed them at the break of day.
All my hopes, all my hopes, were like snow upon the
    mountain,
They vanished like the snow away.

Oh, Coillte Mách, a mhíle grá, we'll linger here a while,
By the shadow of that old Sliabh Chairn.
Roses bloom, roses bloom, all along the Yellow River,
One childlike star steps out into the dawn.

Kiltimagh, Kiltimagh, the dark wind from the mountain
Is searching through the streets down town.
Kiltimagh, Kiltimagh, all your lovely sons and
    daughters,
Are scattered now like the thistledown.

Oh, Coillte Mách, a mhíle grá, we'll linger here a while,
By the shadow of that old Sliabh Chairn.
Roses bloom, roses bloom, all along the Yellow River,
One childlike star steps out into the dawn.

I am so proud of this song. It's the most beautiful of the melodies of all these songs about Irish towns. *Coillte Mách* means 'Forests of Mach', who was a mythological member of the Fir Bolg. He is buried under a great cairn on nearby *Sliabh Chairn*, 'Mountain of the Cairn'.

Some Cover Versions

For a long time when I was writing songs, it seemed that the songs were a bit odd, a bit left of centre, like. Sometimes the lines were not all the same length or the verses were not all regular. It seemed they were quite individual and wouldn't be sung by other people. Then I started getting a few cover versions. What a laugh!

The first time I heard someone else singing one of my songs, it was Sinéad Lohan singing 'The Only One for Me' in the Lobby Bar. What a thrill. And what a beautiful singer. She later released '*Éist Do Bhéal*' (by me and Louis de Paor). Then came Mary Greene singing 'The Land You Love the Best'. Next thing, a great band called The Joyful Mysteries released 'It Wasn't to Be', a really cool and rocking version of it, like. Christy Moore released 'Johnny Don't Go to Ballincollig' on two different albums, and since then he has also recorded 'Magic Nights in the Lobby Bar', 'Gortatagort', 'Haiti', which we co-wrote, and a lovely version of 'The Ballad of Patrick Murphy'. Hurray! Brilliant.

Seán Keane, who is a real, authentic traditional singer, has released three of my songs: 'The Only One for Me', 'The Valley of the Heart' and 'The Land You Love the Best'. Karan Casey and her US supergroup Solas released '*Sráid an Chloig*', written by me and Louis de Paor, and as a solo artist she released my 'We're Going Sailing', and four more songs written by me and Louis de Paor: '*Bata is Bóthar*', '*Buile Mo Chroí*', 'You Brought Me Up' and 'The Song of Lies'.

Pauline Scanlon did a stunning version of 'All the Ways You Wander', first on the Sharon Shannon album *Libertango* and then on her first solo album, *Red Colour Sun*. Pauline later recorded 'When You and I Were True'. Máire Ní Chéilleachair and Michelle Lally also released 'All The Ways You Wander'. Méav Ní Mhaolchatha released 'Since You and I Were True' and 'You Brought Me Up'. Cathie Ryan and a Scottish band called Corran Ra recorded 'The Wild Flowers'. The Battlefield Band, Shanney-ganock and The Outside Track all released 'I'm Going To Set You Free'. Róisín Elsafty released a brilliant version of 'The Poor Weary Wanderer'.

One time I was at a big folk festival in Tønder in Denmark and I heard Mary Black perform two of my songs: 'The Dance of the Cherry Trees' and 'Soon Child', but these never made it onto any of her albums. Still, she sang them great.

George Murphy released 'The Land You Love the Best' and 'The Moon Going Home'. 'Passage West' was released by Caroline Fraher, Girsa, and in a beautiful version by Muireann Nic Amhlaoibh and Danú. Rory McCarthy released 'Ireland Free'. Four Shillings Short did 'I Won't Be Afraid Any More' and 'All the Ways You Wander'. Other singers who have performed live versions of my songs include Nell Ní Chróinín, Mick Flannery, Inni-K and Rónán Ó Snodaigh.

These are most of the cover versions I've had of my songs. It's great craic – always a pleasure, like. Any songwriter will tell you it's brilliant fun to see your work being done by someone else. Thanks, lads! Well done everyone!

Oh, by the way, I forgot to mention, at the same time, like, you can't really beat the original artist, sure you can't!

Near Cootehill Town

In the small green hills near sweet Cootehill,
In some lonesome hollow I will build my still,
Let the silver moonlight gently spill
All around my cabin door,
Near Cootehill town I'll settle down,
I'll roam this world no more.

A mossy blanket for my bed,
The drooping branches overhead,
The rowan berries dripping red,
All along the old lake shore,
Near Cootehill town I'll settle down,
I'll roam this world no more.

So fare thee well, sweet Anna Lee,
I wonder will you think of me

On your slow meander to the sea
From the banks of sweet Dromore,
Near Cootehill town I'll settle down,
I'll roam this world no more.

I visited Cootehill, County Cavan, in 2013 for the *Spillane an Fánaí* series. I used the lakes and drumlins of the Cavan landscape as my starting point for this song, and used an old style of folk song they call 'The Moonshiner'. This is the fantasy of going away into the hills and woods into a hollow where the sun does not shine, making *poitín* whiskey and escaping from the cares of the world. There are verses like this in older songs like '*Buachaill Ón Éirne*' and the 'Rambler Gambler'. These songs about Irish towns have been very well received by the people of the towns, and it will be interesting to see if they catch on.

Castlepollard – At the Very Heart of Ireland

At the very heart of Ireland in the county of Westmeath,
At the lonely Hill of Uisneach, I sat down and I did grieve,
For to see my only daughter flown across the sea,
From the green fields of Erin, far, far from me.
Farewell my girl, fare well.

I've been all around this island, I have travelled near
    and far,
Till at last I came to anchor near the town of Mullingar,
And in lovely Castlepollard I sat down and wrote this song,
Where Lir's lovely daughter vanished like a swan,
Farewell my girl, fare well.

Will ya no, will ya no,
Will ya no be returning?
Will ya no, will ya no, be coming home to me?

At the centre of the island lived the captain of the sea,
And he had one only daughter, so beautiful was she,
'Twas the jealousy of Aoife that caused her for to flee
Like a bird o'er the raging ocean.
At the very heart of Ireland stands a stone so tall,
At the Rock of the Divisions, love will conquer all.
When we all come together and knock the jealous wall,
All will be well on the island.

Will ya no, will ya no,
Will ya no be returning?
Will ya no, will ya no, be coming home to me?

The Irish midlands were unknown territory to me, but they make up a stunningly beautiful part of the country. '*Caith cloch agus buailfidh tú loch*' – throw a stone and you'll hit a lake. Ireland is like a basin: mountains around the edge and lower in the middle. I learned a lot of folklore and history, and met a lot of characters while making *Spillane an Fánaí* for TG4.

We travelled all around Lake Derravaragh, where the mythological children of Lir were changed into swans. It is a swan-shaped lake at the heart of Ireland. I learned that Lir's name in Irish was *Lear*, which means 'the sea', and I wrote my song about him, and I wove into it the story of my own daughter travelling away on the *bád bán*, the white boat of emigration.

Boyle – The Man Who Came in from the Dark

John Reilly was a travelling man from round the town of
    Boyle,
He chanted a store of ancient song of lords and ladies
    royal.
A milk-white steed in the smoky firelight
Went a-galloping away with a golden spark,
'The Raggle-Taggle Gypsy' sang John Reilly,
The man who came in from the dark.
Ring a dum a dero, ring dum a didero,
Ring a dum a dero, ring a dum doh.

John Reilly was a travelling man,
He mended the kettle and he mended the pan,
He chanted the tale of old Lord Baker,
Who sailed away to Turkey Land,
'The Well Below the Valley-o',

He chanted as clear as the morning lark,
'The Raggle-Taggle Gypsy' sang John Reilly,
The man who came in from the dark.
Ring a dum a dero, ring dum a didero,
Ring a dum a dero, ring a dum doh.

Well the scholars and the song collectors,
They could scarce believe their ears,
To hear John Reilly chanting ballads,
That they thought had long since disappeared.
The golden treasure of the travelling people,
Around the campfire glows a spark,
'I'm a Raggle-Taggle gypsy,' says John Reilly,
The man who came in from the dark.
Ring a dum a dero, ring dum a didero,
Ring a dum a dero, ring a dum doh.

With the rí rá ruaille, Mainistir na Búile,
Dream tincéirí, dream tincéirí,
Mise 'gus tusa 'gus ruball na muice,
Rí rá ruaille, Mainistir na Búile,
Fíon agus beoir for the feen and the beoir,
The coonya, the soobla, the rí rá ruaille,
Mainistir na Búile.

John Reilly made a famous record,
A famous record called *The Bonny Green Tree*,
All annotated and collated
By a lovely man called Tom Munnelly.

Young Christy Moore he came down hunting,
And a hungry hunter for a ballad was he,
Recorded the songs of ol' John Reilly,
With a raggle-taggle band that they call Planxty.

Ring a dum a dero, ring dum a didero,
Ring a dum a dero, ring a dum doh.

Here's a health to the people of old Roscommon,
No finer folk will you anywhere find,
To the Grehan Sisters and the old Sheepstealers,
For they treated him well and they treated him kind,
Here's a health to the songs of old John Reilly,
The man who came in from the dark,
To the milk-white steed in the smoky firelight,
Galloping away with a golden spark.

Ring a dum a dero, ring dum a didero,
Ring a dum a dero, ring a dum doh.
Ring a dum a dero, ring dum a didero,
Ring a dum a dero, ring a dum doh.

With the rí rá ruaille, Mainistir na Búile,
Dream tincéirí, dream tincéirí,
Mise 'gus tusa 'gus ruball na muice,
Rí rá ruaille, Mainistir na Búile,
Fíon agus beoir for the feen and the beoir,
The coonya, the soobla, the rí rá ruaille,
Mainistir na Búile.

I was getting good now at writing songs about the towns I visited, and loving the challenge. For Boyle, County Roscommon, I wrote two songs: one called 'Moon Boy', about the actor Chris O'Dowd from Boyle, and another called 'The Man Who Came in from the Dark', about John Reilly, a traveller from Boyle. The chorus uses a mixture of English, Irish and Gammon, or Cant, the language spoken by the travelling people. I was familiar with John's story from Christy Moore, who dedicated his album *Traveller* to him and who learned some great gems of songs from him, like 'The Well Below the Valley' and 'The Raggle Taggle Gypsy'.

In Boyle, I especially loved meeting and playing music with Helen Grehan, who was very close to John Reilly and sings his songs brilliantly. We had great ol' fun on the road in these towns. At the time, it was so full-on that you didn't have time to absorb it all, but I think the craic is captured well in the TG4 shows.

Kells – When Colm Cille Was a Boy

Ceanannas, Ceanannas Mór, Ceanannas, Leabhar
  Cheanannais,
Fil súil nglais, fhéachas Éirinn tar a h-ais,
Ní fheicfidh sí lena lá, fir Éireann ná a mná.

When Colm Cille was a boy he dreamed a dream,
He cast a silver hook into a golden stream,
And dreaming 'mong the holy wells,
He dreamed a book, he dreamed the Book of Kells.

There are four corners to my bed, there are four angels
  overhead,
Matthew, Mark, Luke and John, bless this bed I lay upon,
And if I die before I wake, I pray the Lord my soul to take,
  My soul to take.
Ceanannas, Ceanannas Mór, Ceanannas, Leabhar
  Cheanannais,

Fil súil nglais, fhéachas Éirinn tar a h-ais,
Ní fheicfidh sí lena lá, fir Éireann ná a mná.

When Colm Cille was a man he made a prophecy,
He saw a church full of hypocrisy,
And sailed across the bitter sea, to lovely Scotland,
Of the islands and bells, there he dreamed a dream,
He dreamed the Book of Kells.

There are four corners to my bed, there are four angels
overhead,
Matthew, Mark, Luke and John, bless this bed I lay upon,
And if I die before I wake, I pray the Lord my soul to take,
My soul to take.
Ceanannas, Ceanannas Mór, Ceanannas, Leabhar
Cheanannais,
Fil súil nglais, fhéachas Éirinn tar a h-ais,
Ní fheicfidh sí lena lá, fir Éireann ná a mná.

When I visited Kells – *Ceanannas Mór* – in County Meath, I used
the Book of Kells as my inspiration, which led me to Colm Cille
(AD 521–597), also known as Columba. In this song, I used bits
of Old Irish taken from one of the many poems attributed to him,
translated as, 'A grey eye looks back on Ireland, / Never again will
it see the women of Ireland nor her men.' I enjoy putting colours
into the songs, because people see them, and it was a great
compliment for me the first time I got called a 'painterly'
songwriter. Writing songs is great fun when you get going.

Gorey – A Song for Myles Byrne

When Miles Byrne from Ballylusk came a-riding through
    the dusk,
Upon his dappled mare, there was freedom in the air.
In Camolin and Shillelagh, Casletown, *Cúl Gréine*,
With the brave United Irishmen he learned to march
    and drill,
The men from Forth and Bargy, who stood with General
    Harvey,
Marched their gallant army up on Vinegar Hill.

The ones who fought at Gorey fought for freedom and
    for glory,
To liberate their country, they rallied to the call,
The shackles of religion had impoverished her children,
But the brave United Irishmen, they stood for one and all,
Equality, Fraternity and Liberty for all.

The floggings and half-hangings, picketings,
    pitchcappings,
Upon the heads of Croppies they poured their burning
    crown.
Against the vile atrocities committed on the citizens,
General Abercrombie in conscience he stood down.
The men from Forth and Bargy, who stood with General
    Harvey,
Marched their gallant army up on Vinegar Hill.

*The ones who fought at Gorey fought for freedom and
    for glory,*
To liberate their country, they rallied to the call,
The shackles of religion had impoverished her children,
But the brave United Irishmen, they stood for one and all,
Equality, Fraternity and Liberty for all.

Such hellfire and damnation, served upon the nation,
To hear the pitiful wailing, and the sighs of those around,
To see the people murdered, and see his chapel burning,
Caused brave Father Murphy to turn and stand his
    ground.
The men from Forth and Bargy, who stood with General
    Harvey,
Marched their gallant army up on Vinegar Hill.

*The ones who fought at Gorey fought for freedom and
    for glory,*
To liberate their country, they rallied to the call,

The shackles of religion had impoverished her children,
But the brave United Irishmen, they stood for one and all,
Equality, Fraternity and Liberty for all.

Presbyterian and the Anglican, the Catholic, the
  Mussalman,
The Baptist and the Adventist, the Wailer at the Wall,
The shackles of religion has divided all her children,
But the brave United Irishmen, they stood for one and all.
Equality, Fraternity and Liberty for all.
And bigotry beware, and tyranny take care, and villainy
  despair.
Fág a' bealach, Erin go brách!

After a while I was writing the songs for *Spillane an Fánaí* before
I got to the towns at all, and that was taking away a lot of pressure
from me. Thanks to the internet, I had a world of information at
my fingertips. I came across an amazing book called *The Memoirs
of Myles Byrne*, a description of the 1798 Rebellion by a Wexford
man who was one of the leaders of the revolt. It is a brilliant piece
of writing, and I based my song around it.

Baile Átha an Rí – Athenry

Gold in the sunlight, silver in the moonlight,
Three white swans in the dark blue sky,
Gold in the sunlight, silver in the moonlight,
Flying on homeward to sweet Athenry.

Raghadsa abhaile leis na h-ealaí bána,
Leanfadsa amach iad insna spéartha glé,
Raghadsa abhaile leis na h-ealaí bána,
Fillfeadsa abhaile leis an mbóín Dé.

Raghadsa abhaile leis na h-ealaí bána,
Fillfeadsa abhaile leis an mbóín Dé,
Raghadsa abhaile leis na h-ealaí bána,
Is tabharfadsa faoi fhallaí arda rí an ré.

Rí an ré, reics mar a chasaim í,
Rí an ré, reics fol dí dí,

Rí an ré, reics mar a chasaim í,
Oró is Baile Átha an Rí.

Seolaim, ceolaim na nótaí fána,
Tabharfadsa faoi fhallaí arda rí an ré,
Seolaim, ceolaim na nótaí fána,
Is raghadsa ar sodar leis an mbóín Dé.

Raghadsa ar deireadh leis na góstaí bána,
Leanfadsa amach iad insna spéartha glé,
Raghadsa abhaile leis na h-ealaí bána,
Is fágfadsa an talamh so, an chloch is an chré.

Gold in the sunlight, silver in the moonlight,
Three white swans in the dark blue sky,
Gold in the sunlight, silver in the moonlight,
Flying on homeward to sweet Athenry.
Baile Átha an Rí.

Although we were making *Spillane an Fánaí* for TG4, and I was speaking a lot of Irish, I was writing the songs in English, and it wasn't until I was in the hot seat in the west Kerry Gaeltacht, live on Raidió na Gaeltachta, that this was put to me. I was interviewed by Helen Ní Shé, of whom I'm a big fan, and who is a lovely woman, and she put it to me: why wasn't I writing these songs about towns in Irish? I said that English was the language of the community in all these towns we had visited, and that was why I wrote them their songs in English. Helen said, 'Yes, but wouldn't they like a song in Irish?' She's a great broadcaster and she kind of got me there, like.

I started putting some bits of Irish in the songs then and making them bilingual. Athenry has a huge English-language ballad called 'The Fields of Athenry', and that's what made me follow Helen's advice and write a song mostly in Irish. I enjoyed diving back into the Gaelic to write *'Baile Átha an Rí'*, and I find myself writing songs in Irish now again.

Killaloe – There Was a King in Ireland

There was a king in Ireland, his name was BrianBorú,
He built a golden palace, in the town of Killaloe,
I've seen it in the sunset, the ship of vanished dreams,
All the bridges burning, along the Shannon streams,
The raven from the mountain, the blackbird and the dove,
Meet me by the river, be my river love, be my river love.

*Ard-Rí Éireann Brian Borumha, ar a each bán luath lena
     chlaíomh geal crua,
Sleá slinn sleamhain is a sciath chré-umha, Árd-Rí
     Éireann, Brian Borumha.*

There was a king in Ireland, his name was BrianBorú,
He met a golden woman in the woods of Killaloe,
She played for him such music, the music of the Shee,
It filled him with such longing, the longing to be free,

The raven from the mountain, the blackbird and the
    dove,
Meet me by the river, be my river love, be my river love.

*Ard-Rí Éireann Brian Borumha, ina chaisleán bán i gCill
    Dá Lua,
Rí ar Éirinn is ar thuaidh Mhumha, Ard-Rí Éireann Brian
    Borumha.*

If I was king of Ireland, in splendour and in pride,
I would lay down my golden crown, for to have you by
    my side,
A golden fleet at evening, the timbers all ablaze,
The *Dál gCais* and the *Déisigh*, the Gaelic banners
    raised,
The raven from the mountain, the blackbird and the dove,
Meet me by the river, be my river love, be my river love.

*Ard-Rí Éireann Brian Borumha, ó dhomhan is ó
    dheamhan do bhreith sé bua,
I dtiubh an áir is i lár an tslua, Ard-Rí Éireann Brian
    Borumha.*

It was 2014, one thousand years since the Battle of Clontarf, and
I had the job of writing a song about Killaloe, the home place of
Brian Ború in County Clare. His fort at Kincora, just outside the
town, was his headquarters when he was High King of Ireland
and thus Killaloe was once the capital of Ireland. It's a wonderful
place on the River Shannon, and the folklore and mythology
surrounding nearby Lough Derg is fabulous.

The raven from the mountain, the blackbird and the dove,
Meet me by the river, be my river love, be my river love.

One way of writing a song is to write a poem and then sing it. I have heard controversial arguments from learned professors about the difference between songs and poetry, but as far as I'm concerned, it's all poetry.

Youghal

When we were small we went to Youghal,
All on a summer's day,
The sun it was a golden ball,
The sky a purple grey.
Mo mhúirnín, mo mhúirnín, mo mhúirnín bán,
Álainn, álainn, álainn agus bán, bán.

When we were small we went to Youghal,
All on a summer's day,
The sun it was a golden ball,
The sky a purple grey,
The summer clouds came rolling by,
Like snowy mountains in the sky.
Mo mhúirnín, mo mhúirnín, mo mhúirnín bán,
Álainn, álainn, álainn agus bán, bán.

When we were small we went to Youghal,
All on a summer's day,
The sun it was a golden ball,
The sky a purple grey,
We walked along an endless strand,
Barefoot in the glistening sand.
Mo mhúirnín, mo mhúirnín, mo mhúirnín bán,
Álainn, álainn, álainn agus bán, bán.

I'd like to take you back to Youghal,
All on a summer's day,
And as the evening shadows fall,
We'd walk along an endless strand,
Barefoot in the moonlight sand.
Mo mhúirnín, mo mhúirnín, mo mhúirnín bán,
Álainn, álainn, álainn agus bán, bán.

When I was a small boy at school, we were asked to draw a picture of the seaside, but I had never seen the seaside so I couldn't draw it. I told my mother and she was mortified, so we all went on a big trip to Youghal. It used to be packed with people, but now it's fairly deserted. You never saw such history as what they have in Youghal, between the Earls of Desmond, Walter Raleigh, Edmund Spenser, Oliver Cromwell and so on. It's a really lovely old town. I was happy to go back there and launch my album *The Man Who Came in from the Dark* in Moby Dick's Pub.

Molly Bawn O'Leary from the County Tipperary

Tell my friends that I am well, and playing music in
Clonmel,
I am in the honey meadow, all among the honey grass,
In the shadow of the mountain with my dark-eyed lass,
In the shadow of the mountain with my dark-eyed lass,
We are drinking ice-cold cider from a golden glass.

Tell my friends that I am well, and playing music in
Clonmel,
Well, the first time that I saw her she came shining like
the dawn,
Like a meadow in the morning and her name was Molly
Bawn.

Molly Bawn, Molly Bawn, Molly Bawn O'Leary,
From the County Tipperary, you mischievous dark fairy,

You have me nearly robbed,
Playing on the footpath with your lipstick on your gob,
Molly Bawn, Molly Bawn.

We were roaming in the gloaming, we were busking in
    the dusk,
I played the stack of barley, she played the money musk,
There was music in the mountain, there was music on
    the street,
There was music in the money, tumbling round our feet.

Molly Bawn, Molly Bawn, Molly Bawn O'Leary,
From the County Tipperary, you mischievous dark fairy,
You have me nearly robbed,
Playing on the footpath with your lipstick on your gob,
Molly Bawn, Molly Bawn.

We went traipsing down an avenue of overhanging ash,
She said she'd mind the money, she told me mind the
    hash,
The judge, he said, 'What time have you?'
I said 'It's five to ten.' He said, 'That's just the time
    you'll do.'
And he put me in the pen.

Molly Bawn, Molly Bawn, Molly Bawn O'Leary,
From the County Tipperary, you mischievous dark fairy,
You have me nearly robbed,
Playing on the footpath with your lipstick on your gob,
Molly Bawn, Molly Bawn.

Tell my friends that I am well, and playing music in
    Clonmel,
Do not say I've gone to hell, or languish in this prison cell,
In the jailhouse of Clonmel,
Because of
Molly Bawn O'Leary,
From the County Tipperary, you mischievous dark fairy,
You have me nearly robbed,
Playing on the footpath with your lipstick on your gob,
Molly Bawn, Molly Bawn.

An alternative title for this song is 'The Clonmel Busking Festival Song'. I wrote it at the request of Liam Condon from Tipperary who has often booked lovely gigs for me in Clonmel and has had me at the Clonmel Busking Festival for the last number of years. The deal is you do a gig at night and do some busking in the daytime, but one year I did a runner, like, and skipped the busking. Well, Liam started on to me then, saying, 'Ah sure, that's grand, John, you can write us a song instead.'

The Streets of Ballyphehane

Oh father dear, tell me if you can,
Who are these men who have haunted my childhood,
All round this neighbourhood?
Around the streets of Ballyphehane,
Around the streets of Ballyphehane.

Oh son, oh son, on Connolly Road we remember James
   Connolly,
He was a brave man, he tried to set his people free,
He fought a hard war, against great poverty and
   inequality,
He was shot down in a cold prison yard.
Son, they were brave men, and we remember them,
Around the streets of Ballyphehane,
Around the streets of Ballyphehane.

Oh son, oh son, on Plunkett Road,

We remember Joseph Mary Plunkett,

He was a brave man, he tried to set his people free,

I see his blood upon the rose,

And in the stars the glory of his eyes,

He was shot down in a cold prison yard.

Son, they were brave men, and we remember them,

Around the streets of Ballyphehane,

Around the streets of Ballyphehane.

Oh father dear, tell me if you can,

Who are these men who have haunted my childhood,

All round this neighbourhood?

Around the streets of Ballyphehane,

Around the streets of Ballyphehane.

Oh son, oh son, on Pearse Road we remember

    Pádraig Pearse,

He was a brave man, he tried to set his people free,

He understood that the blossom will fade,

But in the springtime it will be re-made,

And rise again, and rise again, and rise again,

He was shot down in a cold prison yard.

Son, they were brave men, and we remember them,

Around the streets of Ballyphehane,

Around the streets of Ballyphehane.

At the end of 2015, I was invited to a meeting of the Ballyphehane 1916–2016 Commemoration Committee by Maurice Dinneen, a local community activist. Ballyphehane is a suburb of Cork city where all the roads are named after the signatories of the 1916 Proclamation of Independence, and other Irish patriots. I was asked if I would contribute to the celebrations of the centenary of the 1916 Rising, and I volunteered to write a song. I knew that there was a song in the names of the streets in 'The Haan', and I used the device of the father and son conversation, which is familiar from older ballads like 'Dear Old Skibbereen'. I performed my new song in Ballyphehane at Easter 2016, and it was a very moving celebration of the Easter Rising. I was delighted that I was given an opportunity to join the commemoration, and singing this ballad brings up deep and stirring emotions.

Farewell

Well, gentle reader, that's a good bunch of songs for you. I started writing songs when I was sixteen. Now I am fifty-five, and I've written about 200 songs and an opera. I'm starting to get the hang of it now and really having fun. I can feel some wonderful songs up ahead, waiting for me to come and compose them. I enjoy giving songwriting workshops, and I will leave you with some positive advice: Don't turn it into a problem. You can write any song you want.

Enjoy. *A léitheoir shéimh*, have a lovely life.

John Spillane